NETWORK MARKETING FOR INTROVERTS 2.0
USING MINDSET AND MEDIA FOR MAXIMUM SUCCESS

Jenifer Kay Hood

©2016

The 16 Myers-Briggs Types

http://www.myersbriggs.org/

US Population Breakdown

The table organizing the sixteen types was created by Isabel Myers (an INFP person).

ISTJ	ISFJ	INFJ	INTJ
11–14%	9–14%	1–3%	2–4%
ISTP	ISFP	INFP	INTP
4–6%	5–9%	4–5%	3–5%
ESTP	ESFP	ENFP	ENTP
4–5%	4–9%	6–8%	2–5%
ESTJ	ESFJ	ENFJ	ENTJ
8–12%	9–13%	2–5%	2–5%

Estimated percentages of the 16 types in the U.S. population.[29]

"Introverts treasure the close relationships they have stretched so much to make." ~ *Adam S. McHugh*

I've recommended <u>Network Marketing for Introverts</u> to many folks on our team. Jenifer understands the challenges and gifts unique to introverts and her advice and insight on how to build a network marketing business will guide and help both the introvert and extrovert to understand each other. Jenifer explores every angle of business building and I am looking forward to 2.0. ~Tammi Gates, Triple Diamond Representative

Jenifer Kay Hood has done it again with her exceptionally well written, easy to read book dedicated to those of us who are introverts and love network marketing. She has all the right research, humor, empathy and experience to help educate introverts and their extroverts. No more excuses when you have someone like Jenifer to help you along the path to success. ~Susan Nobles

Thanks for being bold and hanging in there when the going got tough and then being willing to share your learnings in this book. Awesome contribution to our businesses. ~Cedar Dietsch

Jenifer Kay Hood has delivered an articulate, insightful book on personality traits and network marketing! Honestly, I left this book envious of many of the talents of the average introvert! We have so much to learn about and from the introverted members of our teams. Especially in the area of offering support and training. ~Anne Korzyniowski

Jenifer's ability to communicate is extraordinary. She has a great sense of humor and her tips are essential for improving communication at all levels. Any network marketing business will find this book a must read. ~ Deborah Meyer

I've been married to an introvert for 20+ years and I never knew all the famous can-do people who are introverts. Our world has been changed by them. My wife and I work our network marketing business together. Jenifer made it clear why our partnership works so well. ~Chuck Gates

Jenifer shows you how to use what most in MLM see as a fatal deficiency and turn it into an asset. This is truly a book for the forgotten masses in sales of all types, definitely long overdue and needed. ~Ed Quillan

Table of Contents

Introduction: What We've Learned 6

Chapter 1: Why I Am Staying in Network Marketing 10

Chapter 2: Why There is Still a Need for This Book 13

Chapter 3: Preparing by Being Your Authentic Self 15

Chapter 4: Social Media in the Rubric of Network Marketing 19

Chapter 5: Using Pinterest® in Network Marketing 38

Chapter 6: How Tumblr® Unlocks Networking 46

Chapter 7: Linking Network Marketing to LinkedIn® 53

Chapter 8: YouTube®: A Whole 'Nother Network 76

Chapter 9: Using Meetup® to Build Your List 84

Chapter 10: InstaGram and Twitter® As Conversation Starters ... 88

Chapter 11: Facebook® and Your Business 102

Chapter 12: Social Media and Beyond 130

Chapter 13: Hidden Avenues for List Building 142

Chapter 14: How to Train Your Extrovert 156

Chapter 15: Final Thoughts for NMI 2.0 165

Susan Cain's Manifesto for Introverts 173

Bibliography: More Great Reads to Help You in the Process 174

Glossary 176

My sincerest thanks go out to Tammi and Chuck Gates for their support and encouragement; Bethany and Michael Gibbs, Susan Nobles, Ruth Little for editing this work, and my team, both up and down lines, for their efforts in helping me build my business. I would also like to thank my upline, Karen, for bringing me into this incredible industry, and all the readers and purchasers of my previous book, <u>Network Marketing for Introverts: A Relationship Guide for the Shy, Timid and Reserved</u>. Lastly, I would like to thank Susan Taylor for her wisdom, guidance and love.

Also by Jenifer Kay Hood and available via Amazon
Network Marketing for Introverts:
A Relationship Guide for the Shy, Timid and Reserved

Unidentified: Three Paranormal Tales (Fiction)

Unstoppable Joy: A Happier You in 12 Simple Steps
(with Ed Osworth)

Coming Soon
Bunny and Vincent:
The Love Story of Edna St. Vincent Millay and Edmund Wilson
(Historic Fiction)

The Glass Nephew (Fiction)

Introduction. What We've Learned

> *If you believe in yourself and have dedication and pride — and never quit — you'll be a winner. The price of victory is high, but so are the rewards. ~ Paul Bryant*

I've learned a lot since I published *Network Marketing for Introverts* in January 2015. In addition to discovering there are hundreds of introverted network marketers hungry for this sort of material (thank you!), I have learned that there are some things I should have emphasized more and made clearer, as well as some stuff I hadn't a clue about. So like a programmer hoping to improve what was already a useful tool, I have decided to embark on NMI (Network Marketing for Introverts) 2.0.

As I pointed out in the first book, network marketing is a $182-Billion-dollar industry that sells everything from sex toys to legal services. Many companies use this model. My company chose network marketing as a distribution method because our product requires some explaining. Many companies choose this model for that reason. Others choose it because they want to cut the wholesale piece — the middle man — out of the equation, so people get a better deal. Avon, Tupperware, Legal Shield, and Mary Kay are all network marketing companies.

Although one out of every nine households make at least some income using this model, most introverts opt out of network marketing because it requires more socializing than feels natural for them.   Meanwhile, extroverts are well-suited to the field because they get their energy from reaching out and usually have a large social network.

When it comes to network marketing (and virtually everything else in life), extroverts want us to model their behavior. They want introverts to generate leads using the same methods and techniques that made them successful. The trouble is, these techniques were designed for an industrial age, the era of the door-to-door salesman. Introverts take years to build their networks. We cherish our little band of eight to ten friends. Our sort doesn't mind long pauses in conversations. We prefer in depth discussions over the shallow reflections of small talk. As a result, we resist the training of our extroverted peers and allow many a rewarding opportunity to pass us by.

My first book, *Network Marketing for Introverts*, explored the ways one can use traditional tactics by adjusting them for the introverted mindset. Even though there was plenty of information to help one get started, I soon discovered there were some missing links, many of which I found in Paula Pritchard's *Owning Yourself*. I wish I had read it before I read anything else. This book makes it so clear what sort of mind set a person needs to succeed. Everyone else seems to emphasize reaching out to strangers and building your list, while Pritchard gives all that with a healthy dose of, "don't do this or you'll screw up your warm market and feel like a failure right out of the gate." I know first-hand what it means to blow through your warm market and I made every single mistake Pritchard identifies. So let me offer a word of advice — as soon as you finish this book and as early in your career as you can manage — read *Owning Yourself!* You will be so happy you did.

Yet even knowing what I know now, I recognize there are still things that are difficult for even the most social of introverts to manage. That is why this volume emphasizes social media as an alternative to traditional network marketing. Sure, there will still be times you have to connect face-to-face, but much of the legwork to find prospects can be done online. This allows us introverts to warm-up cold leads before we have personal contact. It will also allow you to reach far beyond your community to find your "tribe." Instead of pulling business cards off a cork board at Wal-Mart and cold calling people (yikes!), you can join online groups of folks that share your passions, build networks of people in your field, and "talk" from the comfort of your home office.

EXTROVERTS TAKE NOTE: *Why should we build contacts by relying on total strangers? Wouldn't it be easier to talk with friends?*

Many of us have found that we have an even larger circle of "friends" through the friends of friends on Facebook®. We laugh at the videos they post, share what they have shared, and sometimes even find ourselves connecting in person. Same goes for Twitter®, LinkedIn®,

Pinterest®, Instagram and the rest of the social media pantheon. We can "network" without ever leaving our home office — unless we want to.

We don't need to be saved from ourselves, we just need to find a way to be ourselves and connect to enough people to make network marketing work for us. That's what this book is about, offering tools that are natural and doable for the introverted network marketer.

EXTROVERTS TAKE NOTE: *Introverts aren't lazy, stubborn, uncoachable, arrogant, incapable, or making excuses. Introverts are good listeners who are thoughtful, trustworthy, persistent, creative and passionate about the things they enjoy. Don't try to change us. Learn to guide us in how we can use these skills of a master network marketer.*

Those of you who have read my first book may find some of the material in 2.0 is familiar territory, but there is plenty of new information to build upon. In addition to the social media advice mentioned above, I will also be discussing a few things that have really made a difference for me in the past year. Reading the *MLM Blueprint* by Kody Bateman was a revelation. So was reading and practicing *Tapping Into Wealth*, by Margaret Lynch. I advise reading both closely to get the most benefit from NMI 2.0.

Chapter 1. Why I'm Staying in Network Marketing

> *I also believe that introversion is my greatest strength. I have such a strong inner life that I'm never bored and only occasionally lonely. No matter what mayhem is happening around me, I know I can always turn inward.*
>
> ~ *Susan Cain*

In today's corporate world, many people find themselves losing jobs through no fault of their own. They reached the limit the business wanted to pay. They got "too old" to be affordable. A machine took their post. They couldn't move with the company to a less expensive place. The company moved jobs overseas, closed the plant or simply was swallowed up by another conglomerate. I am writing this book because I know there are people like me out there who are faced with making a living in a corporate world that no longer awards a "gold watch" for loyal service.

There is a better solution than improving your "kissing up" skills. But they require you to get used to the idea that traditional employment will no longer fit the bill, particularly if you want work that is stable, rewarding, sustainable, inspiring, respectful, collegial, satisfying, relaxed, well-paid and influential.

As an introvert, working in the network marketing industry was hard for me at first, and still is sometimes. People join your team and then quit. They join and do nothing other than get a discount on products. They become a customer only try a product once and decide you lied about how good it was; or worse yet, they fail to use a product correctly and then blame you and your company for it not working. There are days when it's like watching someone try to make ice cream with lemons and vinegar. It won't work, but they insist you didn't tell them it wouldn't. Arghh!

Nonetheless, I soon realized network marketing is the best solution for a stable, fun and well-paying position — even though there are still days when I want to scream. No one can lay me off. I get to choose who I work with. I have all the support I need. I am paid for my own work and the work of others. It doesn't require a multi-million-dollar investment like a franchise. It doesn't require opening an office or buying boatloads of inventory. It doesn't require insurance. I can work my business in my pajamas if I feel like it. The only things it requires are things that I, as an introvert, have in abundance: persistence, loyalty, commitment and a "can-do" attitude.

With zero prior experience, I have found the right network marketing company. I am building a team. I find myself doing things I never thought I would do. I am a success in network marketing because I created a model that took the most effective tools of traditional network marketing and combined them with what an introvert like me could comfortably do.

Why should you forego millions just because you weren't prom queen or captain of the football team? Thanks to slight tweaks in the original methods and 21st Century social media, even the president of Chess Club can be a success in network marketing.

Chapter 2. Why There Is Still a Need for This Book

Whatever kind of introvert you are, some people will find you "too much" in some ways and "not enough" in others. ~ Laurie Helgoe

When I first got started in the profession, I knew if I couldn't find a solution to the challenges of being an introvert in the field, my business would lose associates at the same rate every network marketing company does. The statistics[1] are staggering:

- In the first year of operation, a minimum of 50% of representatives drop out.
- After five years of operation, a minimum of 90% of representatives have left the company.
- By year 10, only those at or near the top have not dropped out – making it safe to say at least 95% of representatives have dropped out.

If one looks at the statistics under the lens of introvert versus extrovert percentages, it is likely the majority of the 50% first year loss may largely reflect the 35-50% of people

---

[1] http://homebusiness.about.com/od/homebusinessprofiles/a/The-Likelihood-Of-Mlm-Success.htm

who are introverts. Extrapolating from there, one can see percentages might increase as the number of introverts are sponsored. This doesn't mean extroverts never fail or drop out. There are probably other reasons for that happening. Yet I believe if introverts could find a way to successfully overcome their innate predisposition against the "three feet rule" (the practice of trying to connect to anyone within three feet of you), the dropout rate would be significantly lower. Without an alternative to traditional techniques, introverts and some centroverts will fail completely. The time for alternatives is now.

When the "Introvert Revolution" began, more and more books started coming out designed to train extroverts to accept introverts and introverts to accept themselves. Some of these books really do get introversion, some don't. The bibliography at the end of the book will give you a plethora of options that I, as an introvert, did find helpful to a greater and lesser degree.

This book will take what I shared in the first book a step further. As mentioned above, it will explore discovering your network marketing blueprint, why using Emotional Freedom Technique (aka EFT/Tapping) to get past your road blocks can make or break your efforts, and the use of social media and online networking to build one's business and generate contacts. It will show you how network marketing, when employed in an ethical and competent manner, can be an incredible way to build residual income that will outperform other forms of passive income (such as stocks, IRAs, and rental property) and keep your retirement secure.

Chapter 3. Preparing by Being Your Authentic Self

Belief in oneself is one of the most important bricks in building any successful venture. ~ Lydia M. Child

I see it as my mission to help introverted network marketers thrive in their business regardless of what extroverted uplines are telling them. While I went over some of this in my first book, belying the notion that this profession is "just not for introverts" is so important it bears repeating in "2.0."

Introverts are ideal network marketers because they have social skills that network marketing gurus like Eric Worre and the late Jim Rohn would recognize as key tools for network marketing success:

- They are generally good listeners
- They possess quiet persistence
- They are adept at planning
- They tend toward sincerity

We are defective because we approach the world differently than our extroverted counterparts. In fact, if we try to be something we're not, we get depressed, confused or, even worse for would-be network marketers, pushy to the point of being obnoxious. Let's look at some personality traits that you, as an introvert, will find familiar and *how they translate into use as a network marketer:*

- If given the right space, you can concentrate well and deeply. *This helps us stay focused when acquainting ourselves with the product, listening to the needs of prospects and bookkeeping.*
- You often become absorbed in philosophical thoughts and ideas. *You're a deep thinker and not one to dominate a conversation. However, you may appear too deep or too self-absorbed, so watch yourself when developing your networks.*
- You have few hobbies, but those you do have you explore in depth. *You are able to learn all there is to know about your product and offer solutions based on what you know from other people's experience with it.*
- You communicate best one-on-one or in small groups. *This makes you a super network marketer, because it gives you the ability to connect deeply with people, which helps you build a stronger team.*
- You're very selective when it comes to activities and socializing. *Like the quality above, this trait can work for you as a network marketer because it helps you create tight bonds. However, the larger your network the stronger your business, so concentrate on building wide and deep, and if you have to portion out time so you're not overwhelmed, do so.*
- You become drained around large groups of people and are uncomfortable going to parties, especially when the host has invited people you don't know. *This is probably the greatest challenge for the introverted network marketer. Here is where it*

is important to know your limits and honor them. If you are able to say to yourself, "I will go to this party and stay for 30 minutes," you can also give yourself permission to hang out longer if it feels right. You can also compensate for this character trait through the disciplined use of social media.

- You need time alone to recharge. You tend to become uneasy and irritable when you don't have enough down time. *Here is where you will need the self-discipline to quit while you're still functioning positively and will need the support of the extroverts around you. Let them know you may need to leave early if you get over-stimulated.*

- You prefer self-directed activity over group work. *Again, a terrific quality for a network marketer. However, it must be tempered by an ability to work in groups to promote your product on occasion.*

- You reflect back to the person you're speaking with to make sure you're understood — and understanding.[2] *Probably the best skill a network marketer has is the ability to listen well and deeply, then reflect what the prospect needs back.*

Obviously, nothing is absolute when it comes to introversion, extroversion, or anything else for that matter. Some of the above descriptions will serve you well as a

---

[2] *Based upon Hirsh & Kummerow, 1989; Keirsey & Bates, 1984; Lawrence, 1985; Myers & Myers, 1980, as found at http://www.davidsongifted.org/db/Articles_id_10274.aspx.*

network marketer. Others will have to be negotiated around. Nonetheless, the preceding should be viewed as giving you permission to honor yourself when developing your network marketing business and warn you of the potential pitfalls of certain behaviors.

Success does not require extroversion

Today's world is filled with successful introverts. Unfortunately, their success is what makes them seem more outgoing than they actually are. Believe in and trust in your ability to operate your business your way, not the extrovert way. There is more than one way to be a success in network marketing. Embrace this truth as gospel!

> **EXTROVERTS TAKE NOTE:** *Familiarizing yourself with the things introverts excel at will help you guide, support and retain them on your team.*

Chapter 4. Social Media and the Rubric of Network Marketing

When an introvert cares about someone, she also wants contact, not so much to keep up with the events of the other person's life, but to keep up with what's inside: the evolution of ideas, values, thoughts, and feelings.

~ Laurie Helgoe

While social media can be a wasteland of silly videos and who cares gossip, it can also be a means of connecting and sharing the things we enjoy most, which makes it an ideal tool for network marketing.

However, it cannot become a crutch to avoid real time interaction. Personal contact is absolutely necessary at least a few times a year.

Let's explore why.

There are distinct emotional and psychological differences between a traditional business, a franchise and network marketing. All of these business models are being changed by social media. That's because social media and face-to-face contact can provide a "one-two punch" toward success.

How do the business models differ?

Let's say you make incredible pastries and want to open your own shop. You have to find the money to get started, including cash for rent, licensing, kitchenware, advertising, and salaries. No matter how much you think you can do it all by yourself, you have to have staff and all the issues that brings up. You have to find a good location, build up a client base and while you're doing that be prepared to lose money for at least the first five years. I know this is true because I used to work in municipal economic development. Even something that had the phenomenal success of Facebook® took five years to make a profit. This is important to remember for when we discuss network marketing below.

When you go to work as an employee at a franchise like McDonalds, someone shows you how many fries to put in the fryer basket, demonstrates how the timer works, how you avoid splattering yourself with hot grease, and how you season and package up the fries. It's all about a simple system that has almost nothing to do with your family life, your emotional baggage, or what motivates you.

If you happen to be the owner of the McDonald's franchise, not only do you have to know all those nuts and bolts things, but you have a couple million dollars in debt hanging over you. The company will provide you with training, some of your initial inventory, and does all the marketing for you. You have to have insurance, hire and fire people, make sure your restaurant meets inspections by both the company and the community, and pay off huge loans. If for some reason you have a bad location, an unforeseen incident, such as a shooting or an e. coli outbreak, you are toast. You've lost everything. It's bankruptcy city, baby!

When you work in network marketing, you have the advantage of company generated marketing pieces, you have low startup costs, very little inventory to buy, and everyone you work with in the field works for themselves. However, your success will depend on all those emotional and spiritual things McDonald's could care less about. For instance, if your mother told you that you'd never be a success, chances are your self-worth is so low that you find it hard to believe anyone would take you seriously, so making the case for your company is doubly hard, even if you use the tools the company gives you. Your head and heart need to be in the game.

If you're new to network marketing, this may take five years or more. Yes, you read that right. Be prepared to make very little, break even or be behind in the first five years of your network marketing career. There are exceptions to this, but any company that says you'll have a beach front house in a year is not being realistic. The average person, particularly someone who has to negotiate social networking as an introvert, will take between three to seven years to build a profitable business. But don't despair. The same can be said of *any* type of mom-and-pop business.

Please bear with me while I tell you a little story to illustrate the real life differences between these business models.

Years ago, I worked for minimum wage at an Orange Julius franchise. It was not rocket science by any means. Yet, ironically, my boss was a Korean immigrant who had a Ph.D. in nuclear physics. When Peck couldn't find work in the U.S., he purchased a franchise and became determined to support himself with something far beneath his level of education. Every once in a while, someone would come in and say something racist and I would see his jaw tighten as he ignored the slight. But we still made the best burgers in the immediate vicinity of Pasadena City College, so Peck's race and educational background didn't matter to most customers.

Back then if Peck had to go out and recruit students and faculty to come over and try his burgers, and then sell some of those customers on the idea of starting a satellite burger joint half a block away, my guess is he would have had a hell of a time convincing people. For one, he was barely making ends meet as it was. For another, he spoke with an accent that was hard to understand and sometimes people made fun of him. Peck had a lot of resentment about being a Ph.D. stuck selling burgers to a lot of inconsiderate and often ignorant college kids. He felt he was being cheated by his suppliers. His wife was unhappy. He was overweight, stressed, frustrated and broke. Every time a new burger place opened and stole our customers for a while, he'd sink into despair.

In order to successfully _network market_ his Orange Julius business, Peck would have had to overcome a whole host of things that have nothing to do with how good his burgers were. He would have had to learn to be consistently cheerful and optimistic. He'd have to find a way to be secure about his limited English. He'd have to be willing to mask his financial woes, be delighted when new burger joints opened no matter how close they were to his shop, forget that he was smarter than most of his customers, brush off the racist remarks, ignore the doubters who thought Bob's Big Boy was better, and a dozen other things that take enormous resilience and dedication.

In short, traditional face-to-face network marketing isn't something you can just do, like throwing fries into a basket or meat on a grill. It requires — in fact, demands — spiritual and psychological preparation to reach out to total strangers. I don't say this to scare you, but to help you avoid many of the mistakes that both introverted and extroverted entrepreneurs have made. If you think you may need help preparing psychologically for the profession, I go into this in depth in Chapter 5 of my previous book, *Network Marketing for Introverts: A Relationship Guide for the Shy, Timid and Reserved* (available via Amazon in paperback and Kindle).

Suffice it to say that with a franchise you have built-in brand awareness. Someone looking for an Orange Julius will find you because he trusts what this brand offers. With a network marketing business, you seek the customer out even if your company is something as instantly recognizable as Avon, Mary Kay or Tupperware. That's a huge difference that takes some getting used to, but can be handled if you're willing to do some emotional work to keep you from feeling discouraged.

Where Social Media Comes into This Story

The good news is, the reality of finding customers in 1973 is very different than what it is today, thanks to the advent of social media.

In 1973, Peck would have had no alternative to the traditional way of marketing his burgers. An ad in the *Pasadena Star-News* or fliers on a PCC board was about as good as it was going to get. Word of mouth could have made him or broken him. As a franchisee he had to make and sell his burgers at a profit, which meant hiring people like me for minimum wage and working extremely long hours with little reward. His apartment was in a mediocre part of town. The best he could hope for is the entire Pasadena City College football team coming over after practice for burgers. All this would have been true whether he was an independent operator with his own burger joint or a franchise owner. That's just the way it was.

In 2016, if he had lasted that long, he would have been able to take advantage of social media to convince anyone with a computer that he made the freshest, juiciest and best burgers in Pasadena. Then, when potential customers did meet him face-to-face, the connection would be strong enough that Peck's social limitations wouldn't interfere with excitement about trying his burgers.

If Peck's burgers were sold via network marketing, he'd have the added advantage of being able to tell some of those social media connections about how they too could have his company's burger recipe and start their own business. He'd show them the ropes, but never have to worry about how many burgers the downline sold because it would be their motivation that spelled their success, not him having to crack the whip. And for that modest effort, he would get commission from the company on every sale his downline made and every person they sponsored to sell even more burgers. He'd keep growing in prosperity for as long as his team grew. It might take him as long as it took to make the franchise profitable, but it would be his business with a fraction of the debt, hassle and risk.

This is the reason why so many Fortune 500 companies and CEOs (Warren Buffet owns six!), are choosing to add network marketing to their portfolios. They see it as a great way to employ thousands, if not millions, of people without any of the problems and costs involved in traditional staffing. They know that franchises have all these challenges and huge entry costs that place it out of the hands of the average Jo. They can see that the Industrial Age model of the 20th Century of building a strong middle class isn't working as it once did. They create network marketing companies because they know people need second, even third, incomes, but they don't want to deal with the challenges and regulations involved in manufacturing or otherwise working in the bricks and mortar world.

Now consider this: one out of every nine households are involved in network marketing. If every one of those households used social media correctly and frequently, how many people would be touched? Think about it. How many people go to your personal Facebook® page at least once a week to check in on you? What would happen if you said something like, "Just got back from my niece's graduation! She was valedictorian and her speech was just incredible. I'm so proud of the great job my sister and her husband did. I sure am glad I have that extra money coming in from Blank Network Marketing Incorporated. It helped me pay for my car repairs so I didn't have to miss it."

But social media isn't only about Facebook®. Mark Zukerberg's monster platform is just the start of what can be done with social media. LinkedIn® can connect you with people you know in your profession, similar interests, and similar lifestyles. Meetup® can connect you with your tribe. Twitter® makes quick, easy connections on topics of interest and helps generate followers who share your passion. YouTube® allows you to direct people to your company's promotional videos in a less threatening way than telling them to go to your website. And that's just for starters. While I don't profess to know everything about social media, I know what I will share on these pages will give you a head start on discovering ways to build your list that don't involve tackling people in grocery stores or cold calling.

So, now that you understand how social media can change the way you do prospecting, here are some simple rules to live by when using any of these platforms.

Be real: your authentic self speaks volumes
1. Be persistently consistent: Every day is the way. Make a schedule and stick to it. Reliability says you can be counted on.
2. Make sure your content is valuable and not super pitchy.

3. Know the difference between being social and being personal: on your page you can say what you enjoy without delving into too many opinions.

4. Woo your prospects: being attentive, listening well, remembering important dates like birthdays and anniversaries will go a long way toward helping a person feel safe.

5. Pay attention to the rules: every social media platform has them, learn what they are and avoid the consequences of misusing them.

6. Make people laugh: not everyone shares the same sense of humor, but demonstrating you are able to laugh at yourself and take a joke gives you a human touch and makes it easier for people to connect with you.

7. Avoid "same old, same old:" If all people ever see on your social media page is the same old stuff they'll stop coming back. Variety is the spice of life.

8. Integrate online and offline marketing: If you're talking about how wonderful your product is, but there is never a way for people to connect with you personally, you're leaving out a valuable piece of the puzzle. For example, if you're describing how well your product works on skin, tell people about an event they can go to where they can try a free sample.

9. Keep track of your successes: By making note of what works and what doesn't, you'll be able to improve and build upon your successes and eliminate or tweak what doesn't work.

Look at Your MLM Blueprint

There's a wonderful book by Kody Bateman that explores what he calls your "MLM blueprint." Based upon the idea first expressed by T. Harv Eker in *The Secrets of the Millionaire Mind*, Bateman decided that if one could have a money blueprint one could also have a blueprint for other things, including network marketing.

According to Eker, the reason some people have trouble getting and keeping money is because their blueprints are all messed up. For example, say you have a mentor that you really love and admire. She has taught you all you need to know about training show horses and she has the blue ribbons to prove she knows her stuff. Yet every time you talk she subtly complains about her lack of money. Your conscious mind takes in what she says and feeds it to the subconscious mind for future use. Pretty soon it seems no matter what you do you never have enough cash. That is because your mentor innocently made a blueprint upon your mind, and you feel you have to follow that example.

Like the blue prints of a house, you see the outer manifestation of what you were taught, not the inner. Consciously, the blueprint you're following is all the wonderful tricks she showed you for teaching horses, because that is the skill you wanted to learn. Subconsciously, you are also following what she told you about finances, because that was part of her classes. Using the house metaphor, the structure (show horses) may look nice, but the foundation (poverty mindset) makes the entire business unstable.

No one consciously says, "I want to be poor." One might say, "I choose to live a life of poverty," like a monk or a nun, but one doesn't desire poverty. It's a kind of double negative. Yet your subconscious thinks poverty is part of the plans for training show horses, so it makes lack come into fruition so you can reflect the blueprint demonstrated by your mentor.

Based on this, Bateman figured out that people also might have an "MLM Blueprint." They might be reflecting the blueprint taught to them by their best friend who joined the wrong company, or a friend who never made any money, or the news announcer who told them that network marketing was an illegal pyramid scheme, which influenced their subconscious mind. Triggered by their subconscious blueprint, some people have trouble putting the pieces of the network marketing puzzle together. Either they fail completely or never make enough to justify the long hours and frequent rejection. Bateman says that if we can find the source of our "MLM Blueprint" we can repair any of the hidden (subconscious) floor joists and wall studs that are holding us back.

To discover what your "MLM Blueprint" might look like, Bateman suggests that you analyze the following:

1. Your first exposure to network marketing
2. Exposures brought to you by other people
3. The exposure that sold you on network marketing
4. The exposure that frames your concept of how much money people can make in network marketing

5. How you felt when you first joined a network marketing company and your experiences with that company
6. The exposures that shut you down and those that lifted you up
7. And, I would add, your relationship with the person who introduced you to your current company

In other words, "the stories you have in your subconscious are the stories you end up living."[3] Look for the source of your feelings about the network marketing industry. If your original contact with network marketing was a pushy, obnoxious person who made signing up a condition of friendship, chances are you will have a very bad "blueprint" about the industry and not feel good about being in it. If you can trace that source and weigh it against the positive experiences you've had, chances are you will feel better. Sometimes it's that nasty little memory that we've basically forgotten about that trips us up in the present.

Bateman presents some fascinating case studies, such as when a best friend is approached and reacts badly. Her opinion means a lot to you because you love and respect her. This adds to the mountain of negatives you already have in your subconscious about network marketing. You feel hurt, confused and the steam you've been trying to build up for your network marketing engine drifts off like a cloud. If you haven't established a habit of feeding yourself positive, uplifting emotions, this rejection will

---

[3] Bateman, Kody. *MLM Blueprint: Your Subconscious Journey to Network Marketing Success*. Salt Lake City, UT. Eagle One Publishing. 2012. 11

likely stop you in your tracks or at least set you back a while.

Positive emotions are faith-based. Negative emotions are fear-based. Feed your fear and the monster grows. Feed your faith and the angel appears.

Bateman recommends using positive "I am" statements when confronted by naysayers. "I am certain I am doing the right thing. If it's not for you, okay. Some will, some won't, so what? I am moving forward and happy about it."

Look for those things that are creating stumbling blocks to your career and weigh them against what you have learned for yourself. If you have a compassionate and understanding upline, a great product and company, my guess is you'll be able to change your "blueprint" and rebuild that part of your network marketing "house." If all you're having is bad experiences, get Bateman's book, *MLM Blueprint,* and do the exercises therein. They will train you to deflect the negative emotions and embrace the positive, be prepared for people shutting you down, and generate the kind of images that help you stay focused on your goals while building a rock solid "house."

Another Life Changing Technique

Blocks around financial success can be even more daunting than one's "MLM Blueprint."

If you have found yourself repeatedly ending up in the same place financially, I strongly urge you to purchase *Tapping Into Wealth* by Margaret Lynch and fully absorb the insights it will generate. This remarkable book helps you use Emotional Freedom Technique (aka EFT or

Tapping) to let go of deeply ingrained patterns around financial issues. It is not enough to just read it. You should also do the exercises and be real about what you are learning. You don't have to share what Lynch's exercises teach you about yourself. You just have to be willing to let them carry you toward a different financial paradigm. By facing your attitudes around money, you will soon discover why you never made a lot of money even if you were in a high powered, super high paying profession, let alone working toward financial freedom as an independent professional.

Lynch's hypothesis (like Eker's cited above) is that we are programmed when we are very young to believe money is good, evil or neutral. If your parents were always arguing about money you can easily imagine how this would have an impact on a small child. She also suggests that if you were told "money was the root of all evil" and believed it, that you will self-sabotage throughout your career to make sure you're never rich enough to be evil. In addition, if you feel you'll lose friends by being financially in a different league, you will make sure you don't ever have to risk that. In short, the messages you receive both as a child and as an adult will repeatedly keep you from achieving your financial goals.

This is especially important when one realizes that, from a network marketing perspective, the only way you move up the ladder is if you are making enough money for the company. If you believe rich people are all jerks, you will keep yourself from making sales and sponsoring associates. It's that simple and yet it's so deeply subconscious that you need some mechanism to root out those sticky road blocks to your prosperity. Performing the exercises in *Tapping into Wealth* has alerted me to things I had long forgotten about my programming and made a huge difference in how I feel every time I earn or spend money. The book's techniques are too in depth to go into here, but I will tell you that reading this book, doing the exercises and learning "Tapping" will change your economic future like nothing else.

A word to the wise

You can develop a bevy of tepid to warm leads using the very simple techniques found in this and my previous book, but, like everything else related to network marketing, it takes patience, discipline and a hefty dose of faith to push ahead when implementing this 21st Century model of business building. The truth is, you have to prepare yourself to balance steady, consistent effort with acceptance of incremental progress.

Needless to say, this takes some getting used to. It took a long time, but eventually I realized that while I had a load of discipline, I didn't have enough faith. Please sit with that a minute and ask yourself two questions.

1. How much self-discipline do I have?
2. How much faith do I have in myself, my product, the company I work with and in network marketing?

If your answer to these questions was, "not much," you will either have to develop some or let go of network marketing as a career choice, because both are needed to be a success.

You may also find that you suddenly stop working as you begin to succeed. It will sneak up on you. You'll have good excuses. Nonetheless, it will be as if a light switch in what Maxwell Maltz calls your "success mechanism" has been flipped to off. This may be either because you have self-loathing or fear around the network marketing industry itself, or because you have baggage around financial success.

I'm not sure if any of you will find this information helpful, but I'm sharing it because the longer I let it sink in, the better I feel about this profession and the better I do as a network marketer.

As an associate, you will have to muster the faith to move on in spite of ridicule and rejection. In fact, every MLM company expects that level of dogged persistence, but rarely tell you that out the outset. You have to have the courage and faith to work toward your dream thread by thread, without the need for exterior reassurances, including the validation of short term cash. You must have enough faith to take the long view.

Fortunately, we now have social media to help us deflect some of the criticism we sometimes get in face-to-face encounters. Introverts will find this especially helpful, because while we don't mind going the extra mile, we hate screwing up the courage to approach someone only to have a door slammed in our face. Great self-discipline and social media skills can be further enhanced by choosing a company with great tools and trainings that provide techniques for success.

Self-awareness is vital

To be ready to operate your business, awareness of your MLM blueprint, your financial programming, tolerance for rejection and understanding the reason you chose the profession is vital. It is also something that may allow you to make excuses for why you can't do something. Here is where we have to do battle with our habits and embrace improving our skills. We have all overcome things we couldn't do, such as walking, riding a bike, or doing a crossword puzzle. The same is true with this kind of career. If you want to be a professional, you have to stop making excuses and trust that you have every single skill (and then some) required for success. Study after study has shown it, as you will soon learn. Develop a mantra that helps you refocus every time you attempt to second guess yourself. This is mine:

> *If I'm ready to help myself the Universe will help me;*
> *If I'm ready to complain, I have to help myself.*

Psychologist Mihalyi Csikszentmihalyi tells us, "A person has to learn to provide rewards to herself" in order to develop the level of autonomy that leads to self-confidence.[4] You will have to look toward the five-year success "horizon" in between every call and every meeting. Apply every tool for concentration and quiet persistence you have in your arsenal. "Train yourself to spend energy on what's truly meaningful to you instead of on activities that look like they'll deliver a quick buzz of

---

[4] Csikszentmihalyi, Mihalyi. *Flow: The Psychology of Optimal Experience*. New York, NY: Harper Perennial Modern Classics. 1990. 16

money or status or excitement. Teach yourself to pause and reflect when warning signs appear that things aren't working out as you'd hoped. Learn from your mistakes. Seek out counterparts (from spouses to friends to business partners) who can help rein you in and compensate for your blind spots."

Be okay with where you are

The truth is, most network marketers don't start making more than a couple hundred dollars a month until their two-year anniversary. Be okay with that. Don't compare. Work at your own pace. If it takes years to realize your goals, so be it. The important thing is to let yourself be okay with where you are now while also being committed to moving forward.

If understanding your MLM Blueprint, your financial programming, and the need for faith throughout the process still doesn't help you feel better about network marketing, then you may want to find another line of work. But make no mistake, network marketing is not the problem. It is the people or the companies that give it a bad name. As an industry, it is as ethical and legal as any other. It's up to you to do the work necessary to make a success of it, which may even mean finding a different company or mentor. Fortunately, with the advent of books like this one, coaching and social media, it doesn't have to be as onerous as it was in the 20th Century.

EXTROVERTS TAKE NOTE: *Take some time to understand what motivates your downline, her blueprint around network marketing and her programming around money. By doing so, you can avoid exacerbating her fears by making triggering remarks.*

Chapter 5. Using Pinterest® in Network Marketing

Use a picture. It's worth a thousand words. –Tess Flanders

Pinterest® is primarily a visual social medium. You select images — either from their catalog of posts, the posts of others, or your own — and you pin them on a "board" with some remark about what they mean to you.

I have several Pinterest® boards. One is called, "Jenifer's Treasure Map." My intention with this board is to see what I want and visualize those things as if they have already happened. This may sound a little out there for some of you, but "treasure mapping" works if you're consistent with it. On my Treasure Map I have quotes from great writers I admire (this helps me imagine a day when all I do is write), bits and pieces about my product, motivational quotes, photos I have taken, and small pieces of poetry about them, pictures of houses and furniture I like and design elements for a future date when I can have those things. It helps to visualize in order to materialize. Believe it or not, this has helped me sell a house, manifest a new house, a new car and a new desk, and get my spouse to join me in Oregon instead of living 900 miles apart from each other.

But that's not the only reason for having a board like this. You could also visualize yourself on stage as a Diamond at your next convention or large sums of money coming into your bank account from your business. In this way you can establish where you want to go in your business and make social media work for you in a totally different way. It's like the power of prayer. Every time you see it you send a message to God. Every time your friends see it, they send a message to God on your behalf. But I digress...

Using Pinterest® as a marketing tool

Because a complex idea can often be more easily explained visually, Pinterest® allows network marketers to convey the essence of their product more effectively than a whole swath of words.

It's important to be thorough when setting up your Pinterest® account. This includes using your business name, face and logo. Also, be sure to include words that will be picked up by search engines in your description, the more specific the better. You will want to include links to your website and other social media pages in your profile and on the pins. This will insure people will follow you on various pages and enhance your credibility by making you look like a busy and well-connected person.

Pinterest® allows you to have several "boards." You can create multiple boards that would attract your ideal customers. Do some research. What are your best customers and associates pinning? What interests, values, products, and cultural topics would reach someone who could use your product? For example, if your product is a pre-paid legal service, put together several boards. You could have one that would attract families, another that would interest insurance agents, and still another that would entice rental agents and landlords.

Some folks use their Pinterest® board to demonstrate before and afters, post "one sheets" on their products (a one sheet is a quick overview of what you offer), and connect with prospects. As friends and family look to see what's on it, they become subliminally a part of your network marketing world.

With that in mind, it's a good idea to add pins and boards gradually, starting with at least five pins, and build from there over time, adding and subtracting so your board is always fresh. In order to always have that new content, it's important to produce visual content for other sites you're involved with, including other social media sites and your website. That way you can always have something to add to your Pinterest® page and it will attract folks who are looking for visual content to re-pin.

When creating a pin, ask yourself if it's something your likely followers would find useful or interesting, so much so that they would be likely to re-pin it on their boards. Conversely, if re-pinning from another board, ask yourself if they would have an interest in your business and would become a potential follower of your board. If you do re-pin from a board with a huge following, take note of how many times that pin has been re-pinned. If it has been re-pinned by a large number of people, chances are those same people would find your board interesting, thus increasing your odds that you could draw them to your board.

Market research by Pinterest® indicates that 80% of all Pins are re-pins[5], so the odds you will be re-pinned are great and worth the effort. This is especially true if you're hoping to create a presence in social media. If you want to keep track of any re-pins from your website and thus know what's getting attention and what isn't, you can type the following url into your browser: Pinterest.com/source/COMPANYWEBSITE

(Use your company's url in that last part).

For example, I would type the following to keep track: Pinterest.com/source/networkmarketingforintroverts.com .

You may also want to use REACHLI.com for tracking. This site includes tools that allow you to assess how well you're doing with Pinterest® campaigns. It has some very interesting and informative features, such as scheduled pinning (thus allowing you to pin even while on vacation), advertising, suggested boards to follow and best times to pin if you want to reach the right market.

In short, gradual pinning, frequent re-pinning, developing fresh content and tracking results all help you build interest and keep people coming back to your board(s).

Remember: it's not only about you, it's about the whole social community, so find boards that interest you and

---

[5]   http://socialmarketingwriting.com/19-pinterest-statistics-you-probably-dont-know-but-should-infographic/

follow them. Take note of the rhythms of pinning on the boards you are following. Do they post mostly on weekends? Then be there on the weekend to be sure there's a human interacting with you whenever possible. Also, look for boards that reflect the same areas as your product. For example, if you represent Tupperware®, look for cooking boards, food gadget boards, recipe boards, home boards, healthy eating boards, even crafting boards. If you find a pin that you like, be sure to comment about and/or "like" it just like you would other on social media platforms. Scan for boards that are complementary as well as the directly related. Look for your high school, your church, your local clubs, anywhere that you may find people who would be likely to return your engagement by repining something you have pinned.

If you do find that you want to re-pin (share) something onto your own board, it's a good idea to click the source of the pin to be sure it came from a legitimate website and not spam. Once you're sure it's legit, be sure to indicate where you found the pin. This is both courteous and potentially a lead source, as that person might check out what your board looks like with his pin on it. Use @tags to let the Pinner of the source board know you've engaged with his site, and hashtags (#) on keywords.

If you do decide to go with Pinterest®, be sure to edit your pins and re-pins before publishing so they sound fresh, inviting and have accurate links. Use meta descriptions, keywords and tags. (*See the Glossary if you don't know what these are.*) The most important thing to remember is how you are linking with others. If search engines can't find you and people don't refer other people to you, it's impossible to build the kind of relationships that make Pinterest® work as a marketing tool.

Techniques for creating dynamic pins and boards

There are a number of ways you can make your boards lead magnets. Some involve relatively simple things like coming up with intriguing names for your boards, and using clever descriptive words in the captions. Try to avoid trite phrases like "awesome," "state-of-the-art," and "completely unique" in your captions because everyone says their product is that. Use your imagination and thesaurus to really emphasize what makes your product different.

In order to keep your content fresh, you may want to put the "Pin It Bookmarklet" on your browser's tool bar. This way if you run across something of interest while searching the internet, you can pin it directly from there without having to cut and paste urls. By the same token, embed a "Pin It" button on your website, so someone looking at it can directly pin something onto their Pinterest® board. It's also smart to embed a "Follow Me" hot button on your webpage, so people can go directly from your website to your Pinterest® board or boards.

The idea with Pinterest® is not just about pretty pictures. It's about making people curious about you. If you'd like to see a 79% increase in engagement, put a "Call to Action" button in your pins. You might also have a "Call to Action" on your website or blog in order to promote a competition or contest on your Pinterest® board. Make the contest about pinning, re-pinning, commenting or liking.

Add keyword, category and hashtag requirements, or you could have people email you a link to their boards.

For example, say you have a blog and you put a call to action hot button that says, "Click here to enter my *Perfect Pinterest® Page* Contest." The person viewing your blog is directed to your Pinterest® board. There they find an explanation that tells them it is their job to identify the pins they like the most. Then they comment with their email and why they like the pin. The people who comment are acknowledged by you and you randomly reward one or more with a discount coupon of some kind. You now have their email and have learned something about them that will help you stay in touch with them later.

You may also want to invest in creating "Infographics." This is kind of like an infomercial, in that it's dynamic information expressed in a slick, compelling style. The difference is an infographic is an eye-popping visual that just begs to be re-pinned. If you're not good at this sort of thing, have a professional design something that will draw people in. An affordable location for graphics is fiverr.com, where expertly done visuals can cost as little as $5. Another option would be Pinstamatic.com. This site allows you to use templates that help you design "original" pins that include quotes, photos, website clips, audio content, calendars, and maps.

Is Pinterest® right for you?

Is Pinterest® useful? Assuming you're willing to put in the time involved to keep your boards fresh, I think the usefulness of Pinterest® depends a lot on your circle of friends. If they are a very visual bunch who like brief explanations, Pinterest® can be wonderful. There is a word limit to pins, but you could have as many product or testimonial pins as you like and set it up like a catalog. This works best if you're with a company with a huge number of products and/or a lot of loyal customers. You could have a picture of each product, headline description and a link to where a person can learn more. But if you're super busy and your crowd are not browsers, Pinterest® may not be the best social medium for you.

Chapter 6: How Tumblr® Unlocks Networking

Social media sites like Tumblr® represent a fundamental, permanent shift in how organizations and consumers depend on and talk to each other. –Anindya Ghose

When I first heard of Tumblr® I wondered why they had left out the "e" at the end of the word. All the made up words in the social media universe do that to an English major like me. That aside, Tumblr® is a short form blogging platform that allows you to customize colours, fonts, backgrounds and photo placement to express who you are and what you find exciting. You can also include links to other sites using the "Services" tab, select the number of posts you want per page, edit or delete outdated posts, and determine what level of privacy works well for you. This last feature may be especially helpful if you have a Tumblr® account for members of your team and another one for the public. With all this customization one would think Tumblr® was a load of work, but actually once you set it up it, can be configured to pretty much take care of itself, as you will see below.

Tumblr®'s largest audience are younger people between the ages of 16-30. You'll want to reach the older part of that audience. At around 30 you begin to get a glimmer of what the future holds: Babies have been born, school loans need to be repaid, buying a home becomes important. Tumblr® bloggers are discussing ways to earn money, the political landscape, technology, and their careers. You can tap into those needs by directing your micro-blog posts toward meeting those issues.

There are seven different types of Tumblr® posts:

1. Text posts called "Tumblogs" can contain photos, HTML-based widgets, hyperlinks, and videos. You have to be prepared to post re-bloggable content at least daily. Because Tumblr® is owned by Yahoo now, it is emphasizing creating content that is entertaining and loaded with key words and tags so it is sharable.

   You may want to save a draft of a post online and finish it the next time you log onto Tumblr® and publish it whenever you wish. This also goes for the other six types of posts.

2. Photo posts are a single photo with a descriptor and attribution.

3. Quote posts are just that, a short quote and who said it.

4. Link posts consist of a short description of what you'll see and a link to where the viewer can find it.

5. Chat posts are not chats as one normally thinks of them. Chat posts are snippets of conversation shared to make a point. Something like: JACK: *Hey, Jill, let's go up the hill.* JILL: *Why? I don't need a pail of water.*

6. Audio posts are .mp3 files shared with visitors to your Tumblr® page. You can only share one a day, so make sure it's something worthwhile and imminently sharable.

7. Video posts are embedded videos either uploaded from your PC or linked to YouTube® or Vimeo®.

Tumblr® has what they call an "Ask Box." This allows followers and anonymous visitors to ask questions. Both the question and the answer are posted to your blog for all to see. This could be both a blessing and a curse. If they like what they see, they can ask a question that allows you to expand upon what they already like. If they don't like what they see, have a bad opinion of your product, company or network marketing itself, you'll be stuck making a case which can sometimes come off as desperate. The good news is you can turn off the Ask feature if you have to and block people who are obnoxious.

Creating a FAQ (Frequently Asked Questions) and "About Us" post can also address most concerns before they become a problem.

You can also receive and send fan mail. This operates sort of like asking or submitting something to someone for posting, but fan mail is primarily a means of giving positive comments to another person about their blog.

Regardless of the type of post you make, all are rated by the "notes" they get. With each 'reblog' and 'like,' the posts count as one note.

One of the coolest features of Tumblr® is the "queuing" application. Let's say you want to publish a string of testimonials, but you don't want to be married to the computer. You can arrange to publish a string of posts over a period of time, and can choose just how often a new one will appear. You may also schedule when posts are published, so it is more random. This is fabulous if you're on vacation, at a meeting or convention, but still want to keep your loyal followers "on the hook."

Those who post regularly and dedicate their blogs to a certain subject tend to be the most popular Tumblr®s. If you include relevant tags in your posts, people searching for a particular topic are more likely to have their interest piqued and discover your blog. To avoid being accused of plagiarism, you must cite the sources of things you didn't personally create. And as long as we're on the topic, you can protect yourself from people stealing your content and claiming it's their own, by putting the url of your Tumblr® page in the 'Source' box found on the sidebar of the post composition page.

Using Tumblr® as a marketing tool

As you can see from the above, if you have the time and talent for regular blogging, Tumblr® can provide a fabulous way to market your product and build your list.

Fellow Tumblr® users who subscribe to your blog are called followers. If you want to use Tumblr® as a marketing tool, you'll need to get a large number of followers, because whatever you post will appear on their dashboard. Likewise, if you follow other Tumblr® aficionados, their posts appear on *your* dashboard. You can block a person you don't want following you. The more followers you get, the more chance you have of getting your posts liked and even "reblogged."

Again, because this is social media, you need to be social. If you want to contact a fellow Tumblr® blogger, put your cursor over the user's picture on your dashboard. You will see a lowercase "i" in a circle. Clicking on that circle enables you to send asks or fan mail, unless the blogger has disabled these features, in which case you might want to refer to that person's post in your blog, in which case she might visit just to see what you said. As with anything else, be as pleasant as humanly possible. Avoid being too opinionated or brusque if you disagree with someone. Respectful, thoughtful questions will get replies in kind.

Do some browsing to find the bloggers you really enjoy and share that enjoyment. This brings you to the attention of others and helps you share great content with members of your team. If you'd like a refresher on where you saw a particular post, you can find them by going to:

http://Tumblr®.com/liked/by/yourusername.

When it comes to your own posts, remember the old saying, "Brevity is the soul of wit." Short, snappy and thought-provoking posts will get an even better response if there is a great quote or visual accompanying it. Also, if you ask a question at the end of your blog post, a check box will pop up to let people answer your question (unless you've disabled this option). If you're at a loss for what to post, you can go to Tumblr®'s "apps" page and download a "Share on Tumblr®" bookmarklet. This allows you to create a blog post by simply sharing a web page or blog post you found of particular interest.

To expand on what I said above about using Tumblr® as a marketing tool, let me just share one of many ideas.

Say, for example, that you represent a company that develops incredible supplements that improve stamina, longevity and health. That 30-year-old Tumblr® blogger may be looking for you as she notices the stretch marks and crow's feet that are creeping into her reality. She might be posting about finding it hard to keep up with her four-year-old. You might like her page about her daughter's birthday party and share it on your blog followed by a quote from another mother who found your product helpful. The connection made could result in her asking about your product. In her next post, she might reveal she's looking for something that will allow her to work from home. You could comment on her post that you understand how she feels and ask if she wants a possible solution. If she says, "Yes," you could refer her to your blog post about how you made a nice second income selling the supplement she's already interested in. In short, a respectful conversation among peers is started and potentially can result in a mutually beneficial partnership.

Is Tumblr® right for you?

If you enjoy writing and sharing stories, ideas, videos, audios and more, then Tumblr® could be perfect for you to use as a list building device. Unlike traditional network marketing, where you'd be doing all that sharing with a stranger face-to-face, you would be connecting in the relatively safe confines of blog posts. Sure, if that person becomes an associate under you, you'll have to chat on the phone and connect with her at convention, but you don't have to risk walking up to someone you've never known on a playground and ask, "Do your kids ever wear you out?" After all, you already know the answer. Of course they do! The person won't look at you like you're a moron or a stalker. At worse, they'll suss you out as a network marketer and block you from their Tumblr® account. Big whoop! You can move on to someone else who is a little hungrier for the solution you offer. Next!

Chapter 7. Linking Network Marketing to LinkedIn®

When an introvert cares about someone, she also wants contact, not so much to keep up with the events of the other person's life, but to keep up with what's inside: the evolution of ideas, values, thoughts, and feelings. – Laurie A. Helgoe

If you've looked for a job in the last five years, you know the importance of LinkedIn®. This social media platform helps people in the same or complementary industries connect and support each other. It's like a gigantic trade show where most of the participants make $120,000 or more a year. Whether seeking job leads or celebrating an anniversary or new position, LinkedIn® allows you to connect and reconnect with the only people who truly can help you find work or build a new business.

In addition to all the above, LinkedIn® has a means by which former co-workers can attest to your knowledge base, ways to share information, connect with people you know through someone else, industry-based groups and blogs, discussion groups and allows you to post your resume (including short bio and photos of your successes). Consequently, LinkedIn® can be hugely effective as a network marketing tool if you use it ethically and correctly.

Eight Easy Steps to Optimize Your LinkedIn® Page

1. **Create a complete and professional profile.** This includes a professional looking headshot, your title, awards, background, resume, education, mission statement, and make your summary brief and inspiring. A wonderful way to make your website stand out when filling in the "Contact" section is to scroll to "Other" write a short phrase like, "Need help? Click here!" and then put in your url.

   If you've written books or articles or published research papers — or if your company has important and credible documentation (not too many) — be sure to include links to them. You can enhance this feature by having the link be an exciting call to action, such as, "Click here to see why Blank is the fastest growing company in the U.S.!" This will make your publication (webinar, video) irresistible to people checking out your LinkedIn® profile. Your profile also allows you to list your skills. I strongly advise that you only list a maximum of 30, otherwise you look like you're puffing up your resume. Be a strong connector of people and get solid recommendations. In other words, your profile must provide a means of checking out your credibility as a distributor.

2. **Build a Pipeline.** Go to LinkedIn®'s search bar and click "advanced" option. Now you can select just the sort of people you want to connect with. Narrow things down by industry, location and the job title of the possible leads. You can create a spreadsheet using Excel that includes all this and the url of their LinkedIn® profile. Find as many folks as you can, at least 100, preferably 300. Yeah, I get it, it sounds like a load of names, but you're in no hurry and, since there are millions of folks on LinkedIn®, it won't be hard at all to find that many.

3. **Open Lines of Communication.** You want to look like a professional, so don't jump down their throat. Drop them a note that is something like this: "Hi, Shawn, I was just browsing LinkedIn® and ran across your name. I think we both might benefit from connecting. If you're open to that, please reply and let me know a good way to reach you. Thanks, Kevin." If the person happens to be in a nearby city you can throw in something like: "Hi, Shawn, I happened upon your LinkedIn® profile and saw you're in Portland. I'm just down I-5 in Salem and thought it might be mutually beneficial to connect. If you agree, please reply and let me know a good way to reach you. Thanks, Kevin."

When you want to attempt to connect to someone via LinkedIn®, a form pops up asking how you know them. It looks like this:

How do you know Shawn?
- Colleague
- Classmate
- We've done business together
- Friend
- Other
- I don't know Shawn

Include a personal note: (optional)

If you select anything but "friend," you will have to insert that person's email address. Don't feel bad that you aren't a friend (yet!). The prospect won't see that you claimed friendship, and since it's unlikely you know their email, it's the only way you can connect. If you do know the person through an old job, click "Colleague" or "We've done business together" and you'll have to identify where you worked together. If you follow the scripts below, chances are you will at least get a reply. You want to avoid being accused of being a spammer, so go slow. _Do not_ try this with 100 people in a single day. Connect with 3-5, tops.

4. **Create your own group.** At the top of the page is an "Interests" tab. Click there and pick "Groups." One of the options will be "My Groups." There will be a drop down menu that allows you to "Create Group." That brings you to a form that allows you to quickly generate a group that you can manage.

Make sure the group has a snazzy name and get some custom graphics for the group from fiverr.com if you need them. Post a few pieces of information on the group, about three to five pieces so it looks lively and interesting. This can be original content, the start of a discussion, or an article you found interesting. (Make sure you have permission to share and give credit where it's due.) You can find articles at BuzzSumo.com.

Keep the group posts interesting and up to date by checking your industry out on Google News daily and sharing the latest. You will look like a real mover and shaker. Start and participate in discussions, maybe even have some peers participate so the newer folks won't feel like they are the first people at a party.

5. **Invite prospects to join your group.** While you won't get 100% response from the folks in Step 3, you will get a few folks who say, "Sure, let's connect." Your next emails will be crucial. To keep things non-threatening, invite the person to join your LinkedIn® group. If you've taken the time to select the right kind of person, it will seem natural.

In other words, if your group's title is "Beef Buddies," and the purpose of the group is to share beef recipes, don't ask the president of Vegans for Life to join your group.

Keep your message simple. "Hi, Shawn, I'm glad we can connect. I think I mentioned we have stuff in common, so I wanted to invite you to join my LinkedIn® Group. It's a place where members can discuss the latest developments in our industry. I hope you'll join if you get a chance. Ciao!" Again, your response rate may not be 100%, but you will have a means of gauging engagement.

6. **Build a relationship with your connections.** Even if one of the people who said yes in Step 3 does not join your group, all is not lost. The door is still open. Over the next several weeks or months, every now and then share something the person might find especially interesting. Remember the Excel spread sheet I mentioned in Step 2? Be sure there's a column for specific quirks, like if the person graduated from a particular school or belongs to a trade or community group. If, in your daily perusing of Google News, you see something specific to a topic of mutual interest, send that person a link to that information. If that person belongs to Toastmasters, ask if she is going to the Regional Speech Contest. Send them to resources they might need.

    In short, build rapport by proving you are able to build "a mutually beneficial relationship." Over time, the level of trust will grow until you're ready for Step 7.

7. **Write Short Posts.** Brief, informative posts that feature something about your company or product can capture the attention of other LinkedIn® members. Only use this feature when there is important news you'd like to share, like your company making it into "Top 100 of Direct Sales Companies" or summarizing independent studies of your product. Be sure to include a high resolution image, a link to your website and include three tags that will help other members find it.
   The post is sent to all people in LinkedIn who have expressed interest in the topics you choose as tags, so choose carefully.

8. **Connect Outside LinkedIn®.** While LinkedIn® is an amazing lead source, network marketing will not work until you have presented your product to them. If you have been gentle and respectful in building a relationship, it won't seem odd when you invite them to have coffee (if in same geographic area), chat on the phone, or attend a webinar. "Hi Shawn, I hope you've been enjoying our connection as much as I have. It's been wonderful sharing ideas with someone with the same interests. I'd love to take our LinkedIn® connection to the next level. Are you available to chat by phone next Tuesday? If so, let me know when and your number."

Or even more direct, "Hi Shawn, Say, it's been great getting to know you. Would you have time to watch a webinar next Wednesday at 4 p.m. Eastern. The   site   is hxxp://goodstuffmakemoney.com/webinar."
Neither is too pushy, and both help you personally connect. By now the lead is quite warm and there's a level of trust between you. You won't win every time, but you should have at least a few folks that you take through the entire process and, if you've played your cards right, you will not lose those leads entirely. Just give them more time to warm up to you.

Using LinkedIn® as a marketing tool

In your workaday world you meet dozens of people. Maybe they are someone you never learn the name of, like the UPS guy; maybe they are someone you share an office with; maybe they are a boss or co-worker. Like them or hate them, they are potential consumers of your product. The trick is you have to gain their attention without losing their trust – and sometimes that can be a bit of a challenge.

As we saw in Step 2 above, you can build relationships with new people and people you've known a long time using LinkedIn®. I've already outlined how you can build a relationship with a stranger. Now I'd like to offer some possible scripts for people you already know and have connected with via LinkedIn®. It may seem odd to connect with a co-worker via LinkedIn®, but in some ways it can provide a measure of distance and thus comfort. After all, if you're still at a J-O-B, you have to be careful not to tick off a boss by participating in your side business on company time.

So start by looking for people you already know on LinkedIn®. You'll be surprised what you might learn. Maybe they are looking for a new job. Maybe they attended the same university as you. Maybe they belong to the same fraternity, sorority or community service organization. They may even have worked for another network marketing company in the past (siphoning an active and content network marketer from another company is considered bad form). You can establish a time to get together outside of work using LinkedIn® and take it from there.

If you have a wonderful relationship with that person it should be relatively easy to tell them about the way your making some extra cash, whether you're connecting via LinkedIn® or not. If you do not get along, it can be challenging. Let's start with the former and play around a bit with different scenarios that might play themselves out in connecting to that current or former co-worker.

Scenario 1:

YOU: Say, Cris, I saw on your LinkedIn® profile that you're looking for a second job. Have you found something?

CRIS: I wish. My credit cards are killing me and now my car's starting to act up.

YOU: Well, I'm not really sure how you'd feel about what I'm doing, but I'm bringing in an extra $400 a month working part time on my own schedule. Would that help?

CRIS: You bet it would! I only have about an hour or two a day. Is that enough?

YOU: I think so. I'm averaging about six hours a week. I can get you hooked up with my partner, if you'd like to learn more. Could we call you tonight?

CRIS: Before I say yes, what does it involve?

YOU: Let me ask you a question. When you try a product and like it, do you tell other friends about it, like you would a restaurant or a good movie?

CRIS: Yes, I do that all the time. But I'm not much of a salesperson.

YOU: It's not sales actually. It's recommending. If you think you can do that, the three of us should talk so you can understand a little more about the company and the products. Believe me, no one is going to twist your arm and if they do, I'll stick up for you, okay?

CRIS: Okay. You've got my home number. Try calling about 8 p.m. Dinner's over and the kids are settling down.

Scenario 2:

YOU: I can hardly wait to head home. I'm taking my wife out to Chez Hood. We've always wanted to go there and since it's her birthday I thought I'd surprise her.

JANE: Did you get a raise or something I don't know about? Have you seen their menu? That place costs a fortune!

YOU: (chuckling) No, actually, I have this little part time thing going that's bringing in an extra $300 a month. I figure I'll blow the whole wad, but it will be worth it just to see the look on her face.

JANE: Wow, that's more than my car payment. Where are you working?

YOU: From home. What's really great is I get to schedule my own hours.

JANE: Doing what?

YOU: Recommending stuff. Here's a link to the company I'm representing.

JANE: Is this one of those pyramid scheme things?

YOU: No. It's completely legit. All I have to do is tell people about the products I like and I get paid every week. Some weeks it's a pretty nice piece of change, some weeks it's not much, but it's averaging $300 a month and if I keep going, the sky's the limit.

JANE: What do you have to do to earn "the sky"?

YOU: Well, if someone like you goes into business with me, my commission is a little bigger, and if you sign up someone we both make a little more.

JANE: So it's a pyramid scheme.

YOU: No. Those are illegal. You know me, I wouldn't fall for that malarkey. Seriously, look at the video and if you have any questions, we can talk about it tomorrow over lunch. Sound good?

JANE: If it was anyone but you I'd say no, but sure, I'll take a look.

YOU: Tonight?

JANE: Sure.

YOU: Great. You watch it tonight and tomorrow I'll buy you lunch.

JANE: You sure you'll have enough left after taking your wife out to Chez Hood?

YOU: I'll forego dessert if you'll watch the video.

Now let's discuss ways you might approach someone you don't know very well or get along with. In Scenario 3, we'll approach someone you know peripherally, like someone from a different department. Because this person would find it odd if you were all palsy-walsy, your approach should be totally different. Start by suggesting you meet for coffee before work. If he wonders why, just say you respect him and want to run something by him. Once you're at Starbucks, start by checking in.

Scenario 3:

YOU: How's the new department head been for you?

DAN: Okay. He's taking some getting used to after Judy left, but he knows his stuff.

YOU: That's good to hear. You never know when they bring in someone from another industry.

DAN: So what's this thing you want to run by me?

YOU: Well, Dan, I've started a second job with a company that makes hand-milled soap and essential oils and I remembered that you were using tea tree oil on your skin and I wondered if you really think that works.

DAN: Yeah, I do. It's a little expensive, but it's worth it for my rosacea.

YOU: That's good to know. I don't know anything about stuff like that, but the stuff I've tried that my company makes has made a huge difference in my skin, so I was wondering if it was just, you know, the placebo effect.

DAN: I don't think so. The proof is in the pudding, right? Does your company sell tea tree oil?

YOU: Yeah. In fact, we have it plain, mixed with rose oil, orange oil and even with bergamot, that stuff that's in Earl Grey tea.

DAN: Wow, how much?

YOU: It depends. Distributors like me get it wholesale. $2.25 a bottle.

DAN: Heck, at Walmart they charge $5.00! What does it take to be a distributor?

YOU: Not much. I got started for $60, but given the discount it kind of pays for itself over time.

DAN: But I'm not into doing sales. I barely have enough time for myself as it is.

YOU: I get it, Dan. I just fit it in where I can. I'm not much of a salesman either, so I just recommend the stuff that's working for me. That way I know I'm not laying a story on someone. I could give you a brochure if you want.

DAN: Yeah, it seems like it's worth looking into.

YOU: Great. I have a brochure in my car. I'll drop it by your desk and give you a couple days to look it over and then we can meet again. Sound good?

DAN: Give me until the weekend. I'm swamped with the Jefferson project.

YOU: We can talk on Monday morning, if that's better for you.

DAN: Okay. Shall we meet here again? Better not to talk about this stuff at work.

YOU: You got that right! Hey, speaking of work, we'd better hit it.

Now obviously I'm making up names, products, and everything else, but you get the gist of what the relationship needs to be. Casual, but not too familiar. By allowing the other person to lead the conversation and asking permission every step of the way, resistance is reduced significantly.

In Scenario 4, we'll tackle the coldest of cold leads. Why do I say that? Because, in my opinion, someone who knows you and doesn't like you is an even colder lead than a complete stranger. Most complete strangers will at least be polite. A current or former co-worker or boss may be openly hostile. This is, without a doubt, the hardest thing for an introvert to tackle, but I think in some cases changing the nature of your relationship with the person can open a door to better communication, maybe even friendship.

For this example, I'm imagining you looked up your old boss on LinkedIn® and discovered she used to work for a company that's in your product's field, health supplements.

Scenario 4:

YOU: Say, Jean, it's Ryan Durkin here. Have you got a second?

JEAN: If it's just a second.

YOU: I promise I won't take too much of your time. I know you're busy.

JEAN: So, what?

YOU: I need some guidance and I think you might be able to help. I'm thinking of taking a second job with a biotech company that has a product I don't actually understand, but I think you will, since you used to work in that field.

JEAN: What is it?

YOU: It's kind of complicated, and I promised I wouldn't take too much of your valuable time. So can I send you a link and ask you to tell me if you think it's malarkey?

JEAN: Okay, but I can't look at it now.

YOU: When do you think you'll have a chance? You're doing me a favour so whatever works for you is fine with me.

JEAN: Probably the end of the month. The Jefferson project is eating up time for the entire department and I have to concentrate on that.

YOU: Of course. How about I check in after the first? If it looks like the Jefferson project's still in flux, I'll wait until it's done.

So far in this scenario you've acknowledged and respected the person's limited time repeatedly, genuinely flattered her skill as being greater than yours, and indicated you might be out of her hair soon. When you do get back to her, an equally high level of deference is necessary. For the sake of argument, let's assume she has had a chance to look over the website, but hasn't called you.

YOU: Good morning, Jean. It's Ryan Durkin again. Dan Quigley showed me the work you did on the Jefferson project and it looks great.

JEAN: Thanks.

YOU: Have you been able to look at that link I sent you?

JEAN: Yeah, and it looks like one of those multi-level marketing scams.

YOU: Oh really! Wow! What made you think it's a scam?

JEAN: All those companies that sell products with a pyramid sales structure are.

YOU: Gosh, I didn't know that. I always heard Tupperware was a great company.

JEAN: Yeah, but this isn't Tupperware, is it?

YOU: No, but Tupperware's a multi-level marketing company, isn't it?

JEAN: Actually, come to think of it, I guess it is.

YOU: So what was the thing that made you think the biotech company is a scam. I don't want to be taken in.

JEAN: For one thing, I've never heard of them.

YOU: I see. On the other hand, technology is always changing and new companies start all the time. In fact, before Mr. Huston started Digitech, nobody heard of it and yet here we are. Was there anything else?

JEAN: Not really, I just know so many people who got started with one of those companies and ended up with a garage full of junk they can't unload.

YOU: I don't think that's true with this company, but I've heard that too. Let me do some more digging and I'll let you know what I find out if you're interested.

You notice that I did not suggest getting Jean on a three-way call or suggested another website. I acknowledged her concerns, gently countered her arguments, and left the door open. People like this need finesse.

Look for the real reason they are resisting. When a person says no to network marketing, it is usually because they or someone close to them has had a bad experience in the industry. Ask questions. Draw people out. Listen deeply and compassionately. Find the reason behind the reason.

Then do not try to convince, just illustrate why you are happy with the industry. Share your why. "I get it. It can be very hard for some people. For me it's worth it because I get a chance to change lives for the better. That's the main reason I'm doing it." If one of your motivators is making extra dough, don't talk about that. Talk about what that extra money allows you to do without being obnoxiously flashy, which will only translate into unbelievable.

For example, the additional cash let you pay off your student loans, gave you a way to save for retirement, or allowed you to chip in for your granddaughter's summer camp. Then sit back and listen. Be gentle. Keep them informed. See if they're willing to try product alone. But never, ever push them to be associates. They have to make that decision on their own, and the only way they can make it is based on what they see you doing and receiving.

Now for one final scenario, and this one is specifically geared toward what might happen if you connected with a stranger via LinkedIn®.

Because of the way LinkedIn® works, your initial contact will be finding someone in a similar or complementary field. This is not an invitation to another network marketer, by the way. That is considered bad form. Instead, find someone who is in a field related to your product. LinkedIn® asks you to identify how you know a person, and so if you don't know him at all, you'll have to purchase a premium membership. This total stranger will have to approve of the connection before you can even drop him a line.

For this scenario, we'll imagine your product is make-up and you have found someone who is an aesthetician. While this person may be peripherally related to someone you know, say, for example, your hair dresser, this dialogue is with someone who has already allowed you to "link in" with her even though she doesn't actually know you. You've arranged a phone call via LinkedIn®'s InMail service.

Scenario 5:

YOU: Hi, Pat. This is Bobbi Durkin. We arranged for a short chat today. Is this still a good time?

PAT: Yes. I have about five minutes.

YOU: In that case, let me cut to the chase. Are you happy with the mascara products you're using and carrying?

PAT: I'm pretty happy, yeah. I just wish I didn't have to worry about the mark-up.

YOU: I understand your dilemma. Places like Walgreens have the market pretty well sewn up and the products stink. Are you open to an alternative?

PAT: I suppose.

YOU: In the interest of honouring your time frame, I'm going to send you to a website to look at the products I represent. When do you think you'll have a chance to take a look?

PAT: I do all that sort of thing on Tuesday morning.

YOU: Okay, so if I called you on Wednesday you will have had a chance to look it over?

PAT: Yeah, unless something gets in the way.

YOU: Sure, I understand. You never know what can pop up when you run your own business or with the family. Is there a good time to call on Wednesday?

PAT: I'm usually pretty slow around 10:30.

YOU: I'll put that in my book and get back to you then. Thanks for your time. Have a great day.

As you can see, in this scenario the emphasis was on making sure Pat's time was honored. Honoring a prospect's time is paramount when you don't know someone. Naturally, it is possible Pat would ask what brand you represent, in which case you would reply, but otherwise keep it short. If Pat says, "I tried that brand a few years ago and the mascara was super gloppy and irritated people's eyes," you want to acknowledge her misgivings. If you can honestly say, "Yes, XYZ Brand heard those complaints and completely redid their formula," then do. Otherwise, thank Pat for her time and get off the phone. You can try again later with, "I checked with my lead distributor and he says those problems have been addressed." If the formula is the same as it's always been, leave it alone and move on. You want to keep your name free of the stain of seeming too pushy.

Professional Associations and LinkedIn®

Consultant T.R. Garland says the key to success with LinkedIn® is to "Be Visible, Be Vocal and Be Valuable."[6] Now I already explained how you can do those things, but just to refresh your memory, you can "Be Visible" by making sure your profile is complete; you can "Be Vocal" by joining groups, being active and reaching out to new and old friends and co-workers; and you can "Be Valuable" by sharing job leads, recommending others and participating in groups.

---

[6] http://www.leveraginglinked.in/

Now I would like to briefly discuss using LinkedIn® as a means to raise your profile with professional groups, such as the International Brotherhood of Electrical Workers, local bar association or whatever.

Many of these groups have monthly, quarterly or annual meetings that need speakers and presenters at those events. You can use LinkedIn® to connect with officers and suggest presenting at an upcoming meeting.

Similarly, many of them have newsletters. You can find out who you would submit an article to and reach their entire membership.

Depending on the nature of the organization, you can join and attend those meetings and perhaps even volunteer in some capacity. These groups often have special events where they need people to set up or tear down, operate a cash register, sign people in or present on some topic or another.

If you are unable to join the group you're interested in, you can get the name of officers and find other ways to reach them. You will want to tread lightly because this is most likely a total stranger, and LinkedIn® frowns on trolling and spam. A quick note via text message or InMail that reads something like: "Hi, Joe. I work with a company that makes widgets specifically designed to help IBEW members perform electrical work more safely. If you have any interest in learning more, please contact me at 123-456-7890. If you do not want to be bothered, simply ignore this message. Thank you."

Is LinkedIn® right for you?

If you've had a solid career and have a little imagination, LinkedIn® can be a God-send. Chances are there are hundreds of people who will be familiar with your name, introvert or not. These people will welcome hearing from you. Throw in school chums, people in similar or complementary fields to your product and there are literally thousands of people you can reach.

The importance of rolling out the red carpet for visitors to your LinkedIn® "trade show booth" cannot be overstated. Make your LinkedIn® page as complete as possible. It is the only way people can find you and the primary way you will be able to reach those unknown connections who have been searching for your product. Respond immediately to queries, post, share and recommend. Make yours look and feel like the coolest booth out there.

This requires visiting your page frequently to change small things, like your background, head shot, rank or other things. LinkedIn® will send a notice about the updates to the people you're connected with whenever you do this, which increases top of mind awareness. This will give show prospects that you're making progress in your career and capture some of your excitement about the network marketing industry.

> EXTROVERTS TAKE NOTE: *You can help your downline by posting a flattering recommendation on their LinkedIn page and making sure you're connected. People who have many connections are more attractive, especially to cold prospects.*

Chapter 8. YouTube: A Whole 'Nother Network for Marketing

Not only has volume been ratcheted up but expectations have, too. Quiet success — painting a picture, writing a poem, writing an algorithm — is all well and good, but if you haven't become famous doing it, then did it really matter? – Sophia Dembling

Sometimes I ask myself, "Do I really need more TV?" The answer is sometimes jarring, akin to, "Hell, no." Other times the answer is gentler, like, "If it's meaningful." So as I begin this discussion of YouTube® my first question to you is, "Can you build a meaningful online television channel?"

I can't tell you how many hours I have spent trolling this hybrid of television and social media for something interesting, fun or related to my product. Naturally, I get caught up in videos about subjects that fascinate me, such as ghosts, UFOs, TED Talks, ancient civilizations, when all I really went there for was a video about my product that someone recommended. So a word of caution: Use a timer when watching YouTube or you'll watch an entire work day go down the tube (pun definitely intended).

If you think you can build a channel worth watching, YouTube® can be a wonderful tool for getting your message out there. Testimonials, product demonstrations, how-to, training modules and comparisons can make a powerful testament to your product. Since I have already illustrated how easy it is to get caught up in watching videos, if your channel is filled with material that begs the viewer to watch just one more, chances are YouTube® is for you.

Building a Channel

Creating a YouTube Channel starts with your approach. Are you able to "turn on" the happy "talking head' effect of a news reporter? Are you more interested in becoming a funnel for videos other people make? A combination of the two?

Here are some thoughts about the former. Be certain that you have a decent webcam and microphone set up. Make sure your lighting is either natural or directly toward you, so there are no pesky shadows to spoil the illusion of a "professional" video. Create a nice backdrop. There is nothing that spells unprofessional more than a cluttered room with kids toys and a dog wandering through. Put the dog outside, get one of those folding room dividers, and dress for success. If nothing else, make sure the camera is at eye level, not looking up your nose. Maybe put a curtain behind you if you don't have a room divider.

Sit in a comfortable chair with your hands folded nicely in front of you as you start your "broadcast." Use simple, direct language and have your speech somewhat memorized. There's a fine line between sounding phony and too practiced and seeming too casual. You'll want to straddle it.

"Good afternoon! My name is Jenifer Kay Hood and I would like to bring you up to date with my product. Recent studies indicate..."

You see what I mean? I've used my name. I'm talking in a friendly but slightly formal style.

So let's say your company has an incredible new video out. "Hi! This is Jenifer Kay Hood. This is just a short introduction to a video that's going to show you why I am so excited about my company. I especially find the new information at minutes 2-5 in the video super inspiring. Enjoy and be sure to call me at 123-456-7890 if you'd like more details."

Again, I have been friendly, brief and set up what I really want them to see. This is particularly helpful when the new company video has the same old, same old in the first two minutes of the video. People will turn off the channel. They'll say, "Oh, I've seen this before." They will appreciate your sensitivity if you indicate the parts that are the most important for them to watch.

If you decide to forego the role of talking head, have your picture, name and a short bio on your channel at the very least. Spend some money getting a decent picture taken. Don't use an avatar, flower, or out of focus, cropped shot from your Aunt Sally's wedding. Your photo doesn't have to be super formal, but it does need to show you at your best.

If you want to use a video by someone else, be absolute certain you have permission to use it. YouTube has some very finely nuanced legal language that takes them completely off the hook if you decide to violate someone's copyright. So ask and keep a record of asking. It's probably okay if your company is sending the video out, but it's perfectly sensible to have a "CYA" file. (The C stands for Cover. The Y stands for Your. You'll just have to sit with what the A stands for.)

This social media site is cracking down on network marketers. Consequently, you have to exercise caution and not just make extended commercials. Content must reflect another interest unrelated to your product and not refer people to your sales page. That being said, creating a YouTube® Channel is easy and fun. Either you can post your own videos — which I recommend if you feel comfortable doing so — or you can post those of others. There's space for blogging and comments about the videos. The videos should be under 14 minutes, but may be longer with permission. You must have the copyright to those videos if over 14 minutes, and videos you share from others must be given an acknowledgement.

For example, I might put a friend's video about mountain biking up and say, "Video courtesy of Randy Dreiling." Then I can talk about how my product improves one's stamina and the various professional cyclists who are using it as part of their training regimen. I might even film myself giving a testimonial, or talking about my week.

The important thing is — as much as your skill will allow — make these home videos more than just talking heads. Try generating before and after videos of yourself. Film events. Tell a story with pictures and music. As long as these are short — ideally between three and five minutes — you'll get plenty of hits when someone goes to YouTube® and types in key words related to your product. This makes people anxious to see your site and learn what's new.

Using Your Company's Channel

As I pointed out above, you need permission to use things copyrighted by others. Using videos found on your company's channel usually implies consent, except in the following cases:

1. You make claims about your product that are not supported by evidence.
2. You contradict the information your company is giving.
3. Your company expressly forbids the dissemination of their YouTube site or use of the YouTube site for linking on other social media pages or any other website, including your own.

Obviously, when in doubt, ask. It is better to have a paper trail showing you made an effort to be compliant than just willy-nilly post a video anywhere.

> **EXTROVERTS TAKE NOTE:** *If you've always dreamed of being Anderson Cooper, you may want to suggest being the face of your downline's YouTube® channel. You will still get the benefit of any business they get and you may save them from getting so far out of their comfort zone that they waste time and energy trying to be someone they're not.*

Employ Caution When Commenting

Regardless of how you use YouTube®, be careful with your language. Bad mouthing your competition or arguing with someone about their opinion on your post is not only a waste of time, but potentially dangerous. Whatever you say should be polite, respectful and supportive. If your competition says, "That's bunk," you can delete that post. If a teammate writes, "If you like this product, go to Mywebsite.com," delete the post and put your own down. If someone says, "I own the copyright on this music/video," immediately delete the post and send that person an apology.

How Useful is YouTube®?

Having your very own channel is potentially incredible, but it requires a lot of work. When Oprah Winfrey started her OWN television network, she was astounded at how much more complicated it was than running a huge syndicated talk show.

You have to be aware of possible copyright infringement, libel issues and all sorts of other legal entanglements. The content always needs to be fresh and updated whenever new information is available. Production values have to at least make viewing enjoyable and interesting.

That's why I recommend taking the fullest advantage of your company's YouTube channel. If you feel you just must have your own channel, I advise getting permission from your company to simply repost anything they do. You eliminate much of the risk involved by doing this, as the company has gangs of highly paid lawyers making sure whatever is posted is accurate and as risk free as possible. Then keep your comments to a minimum and make sure they are compliant.

All sorts of people have made money by having an awe (or ahhh)-inspiring video on YouTube®. If positioned correctly, a video might encourage someone to look you up. For example, I recently looked up how to tie a knot in a picture frame wire. The video this framing shop offered was fun, easy to follow, and invited me to contact them if I needed more assistance. I didn't, but a friend of mine didn't want to mess with framing her own pictures, so I recommended them to her.

You can do something similar. Say you're a cosmetic representative. You could post a video on, "How to Choose the Colour That's Right for You." Include your website address and phone number somewhere in the video, and be sure to use key words like complexion, skin, colour palette, etc. in your set up. If the video is informative and offers a free colour consult to viewers, chances are you'll get some outreach.

Chapter 9. Meetup to Build Your List and Promote Your Product

You don't start out saying, "I'm going to build the biggest, baddest wall ever made. You start out laying the first brick as perfectly as you can. — Will Smith

Meetup® is a weird hybrid between social media and a dating site. One starts employing this fabulous resource by going to Meetup®.com and putting in your location, how far you're willing to drive and what sort of activities most interest you. This is why it is perfect for introverts. We're not going to be expected to fake enthusiasm for things we could care less about.

Introverts are likely to have a small circle of friends, so joining groups is a great way to build your list. Do not think of these groups as solely a means to an end. Think of them the way you would if you moved to a new town and wanted to find a place to socialize, practice your faith, or play a round of golf. When you're only there to make money, people will quickly suss that out. When this happens you lose trust, and trust is essential in this business.

It's wise to look for events that are close to where you live. If events require you to drive into neighborhoods you don't like being in or at times when you're asleep, you'll be less likely to attend them. Nearby events make it harder to have an excuse to flake out (something introverts are notorious for because we get so uncomfortable with groups). Start attending events regularly. You'll meet a bunch of like-minded people that will be easy to talk to because you already have so much in common. The bonds created are genuine and sincere because you start from a place of wanting to *know* more people, not because you wanted to *sell* to more people.

When I'm at a meeting and someone asks me what I do, I tell them, "I represent a company that is revolutionizing health care." This gets their attention. In time, an opportunity will present itself to tell them about my product. This is why it may take a while to build your business. You don't just go to an event and vomit your story all over people. You go, socialize, and then present your product in a quiet but confident way, just as you would to any new friend.

You may also want to create your own events. I must confess I have found this is somewhat easier for me than groups started by someone else. I feel more in control. I can have the event when I want to, control the number of people who attend, and where we meet. I have also found that over time people in my groups begin to suggest locations and times that I am perfectly comfortable with. You participate when and where you want. If your Movie Lovers group wants to see a movie you've already seen, you can back out with no loss of face or regret.

How to appropriately bring up your business

Let's say the group is talking about the things going on in their lives. Someone says, "Yeah, my family is dealing with [something related to your product]." You nod and listen attentively. You genuinely sense your product may be a good fit for the situation. You might ask something like, "What have you tried?" Notice that I didn't say, "Have you tried Blank?" Using the latter approach, usually results in people pricking up their ears like deer in a field when a hunter approaches. By asking a "what" question you are leaving the door open for them to talk more about themselves.

The important thing to do is establish what their "pain" is and not try to address it unless you genuinely think your product will help. You have to be fully present for people to feel safe, and if all you're doing is looking for an opening to sell your product you will quickly lose any new connections you've made. The longer you can sustain a friendship, the more intimate and close you become with people. The closer you are to a person the more likely she will be to take your advice. It may take a while to develop this sort of closeness, but it is much more sustainable that bullying someone into buying your product.

Already people in my Meetup® groups have purchased products from me and some are even considering joining as associates. They did so because I genuinely offered an empathetic ear and a loving heart to address their needs, not because I pushed my product or agenda.

EXTROVERTS TAKE NOTE: *As much as possible, attend the Meetups your introverted downline starts, but resist the urge to take over. Your role is to support her by being a "butt in a chair."*

Chapter 10. Instagram and Twitter as Conversion Starters

Brevity is the soul of wit. — *William Shakespeare*

If you want to reach a younger audience of Gen X or Millennials, you'll have to become acquainted with Instagram® and Twitter®. The wonderful thing about this demographic is they specifically are looking for home-based, relationship-based self-employment. This makes them natural network marketers, particularly if they have a day job, parents or friends they can live with, and a resilient work ethic.

Think of these two platforms as conversation starters. They will not make the whole sale for you, but they will exponentially build your list and create interest in your product if you work them right. Both are designed for quick bursts of information. Think the office water cooler or pictures in your wallet. You can't tell the story of your life at the water cooler if you want to keep your job, and you can't explain how you met your wife by opening your wallet to show her picture. However, you can say, "I've got a great part time job. Would you like me to send you a link?" or "This is my beautiful wife Jane and these are our great kids, Sally and Dick."

What is Instagram?®

Is your product something that has to be seen to be believed? If so, Instagram® is right for you. Used primarily by people 20-30, this can be the most effective brand-building tool in your social media arsenal.

Instagram® is primarily a visual medium. People post images with very short commentary. The idea is a "picture is worth a thousand words," so there's no need to be verbose. Just offer a minimal explanation of what a person is seeing.

Forrester Research, an independent arbiter of technology effectiveness, calls Instagram, "the king of social engagement."[7] They discovered that major companies achieve a per-follower engagement rate of 4.21, or put another way, Instagram® delivered 58 times more engagement per follower than Facebook®, and 120 times more engagement than Twitter®![8]

How to use Instagram as a marketing tool

You're going to want to start by checking out what businesses are doing really well with Instagram® and take notes. What are they doing well? What are people attracted by? Are there any competitors you should be learning from? How can you emulate what they are doing and still speak with an individual enough voice that you look original?

---

[7]   http://blogs.forrester.com/nate_elliott/14-04-29-instagram_is_the_king_of_social_engagement

[8] Ibid

Now, look at your goals. Are they S.M.A.R.T. (Specific, Measurable, Attainable, Relevant and Time-based)? Decide exactly how you're going to approach your outreach efforts. How will you know if your efforts are successful? Are you biting off more than you can chew? Do they make sense given your product? How long are you going to give yourself to reach them?

For example, if I said, "Network Marketing for Introverts is a company run by a former corporate communications officer with an interest in music and art who also writes fiction while helping introverts and extroverts do a little better sometimes. The owner hopes to be a millionaire next week," I would be far off the mark of being S.M.A.R.T. However, if I said, "This year Network Marketing for Introverts will help 100 introverted entrepreneurs achieve a rise in rank within their first year in business by providing advice on how to build on their strengths by utilizing their unique talents to manage, sustain and develop their business with a goal of achieving a ten-fold increase in revenue," I would have outlined a goal that is specific (provide introverted entrepreneurs a means to build on their talents to manage, sustain and develop their business), measurable (100 introverts), attainable, realistic and time based (this year).

Now that I know my goals, my next step is generating a mission statement, which is basically a variation on my goal statement: "Network Marketing for Introverts is dedicated to helping introverted entrepreneurs achieve a rise in rank within their first year in business by providing advice on how to build on their strengths by utilizing their unique talents to manage, sustain and develop their business."

With my goals and mission statement in mind I will now plan:

- How often to post
- The best time of day to post to be consistent
- My content calendar
- My content themes

I don't want to overwhelm my followers, but I don't want them to be bored. A safe bet is one to three posts a day, so I decide on two. Next, I need to determine what is the best time to post. I start by looking at what my competitors are doing and I post either slightly ahead of or behind them. Then I consider what sort of response I'm getting. If I get zero response at three in the afternoon, it makes sense that I will go later because the average working stiff is beginning to flag just before the end of the day and may want a quick diversion. I might also notice that early morning posts are viewed well, so I set my content calendar for twice a day: 7 a.m. and 4 p.m. If adhering to this reliable schedule is too onerous, sign-up with Hootsuite®'s Instagram® tool so you can set the schedule and let Hootsuite® do the posting for you.

My content should rely on my theme colours, fonts and layout style. Visitors to my website will know that I love russet orange. But since I want to establish a particular look, one that will say *Network Marketing for Introverts* at a glance, I will combine that lovely deep orange with black and a lapis blue for accents. My font will be Franklin Gothic. It's easy to read and somewhat unique visually. I like a clean, easy to navigate style, so my layouts will reflect that. Now I will be instantly recognizable as a brand.

Chances are your company uses specific colours, so ask what the shades are. This is called the RGB (the percentage of Red, Green, Blue pigment in the mix). If they can't or won't tell you (some colour mixes are proprietary so they are a closely guarded secret by marketing departments), find a colour that comes the closest to what the company is using by Googling the name of the colour. For example, the RGB of lapis is 37 Red, 97 Green and 156 Blue. If you're not sure of the colour, just Google, "shades of blue," and you'll find it or something close.

If I have a follower who sends me a photo of herself holding up her pin for becoming Bronze with her company, I will make sure that I credit her. I could do that two ways. I could say, "My client Betty Smith shows off her Bronze XYZ Brand pin," or I could leave out the words XYZ Brand altogether. I will let Betty decide. The last thing I want to do is get her in trouble with her company. To be safe, I may only post her photo if she includes a short testimonial under her picture.

User generated content like this can really work for you if it is interspersed with product photos. For example, if there was a picture of me leading a class, and a woman (shot from behind) raising her hand, and this picture is beside the testimonial picture of Betty Smith, the reader will make the inference that the woman in the picture and Betty are the same person and decide attending a class of mine will be worth the trouble.

All this may sound cynical, but the fact is, sales of any type is designed to help people make associations. "You're in good hands," tells people their insurance company will carry them. Whether it's true or not is debatable, but people make the association and choose the company or not based on how believable the connection is. This is something worth bearing in mind as you develop your Instagram profile and choose your colours, fonts and style. If you're selling legal insurance and your page looks like a gangster is promoting it, people will be wary.

Your user name should match the one you use on other platforms as much as possible. If you can (some companies won't allow this), make all your social media pages have the name of your product as part of your user name. For example, Jenifer XYZBrand. Don't forget to include your website in your 150-character bio. Explain that you "represent XYZ, that they make the best widgets and sell them through relationship marketing." Just that phrase in quotations above is 92 characters, so you may need to leave out http, www and the rest of that stuff before your actual company name or use MLM instead of "relationship marketing."

For your profile picture, use a photo of yourself wearing something that identifies you as a representative of XYZ.

It is common for people to forget to set up their notifications. You'll want to enable both "Like" and "Comment" notifications because they are critical to engagement with your followers. If someone tags your brand, you will be notified if you enable "push notifications." Make sure any user-generated content is acknowledged and appreciated. Don't worry, you can delete anything that steps on your toes.

Finally, start following other people and ask your followers in other social media to check out your Instagram® page. Find key people in your industry, customers, prospects and complementary fields that you can engage with. Make a point of commenting on other people's photos and congratulating people on their achievements. Needless to say, you don't want to counter a competitor's before and after with one of your own. Keep it positive.

Instagram® has an analytics feature that helps you keep track of the performance of your posts. Use it to establish what you want to track and how often you want the data mined. I recommend setting it up so you know where you stand weekly. This way you'll know what images are inspiring followers and which aren't, so you can put more of the former and less of the latter as time goes by. If there's an image that you really like but which doesn't seem to be getting any traction, try changing the accent colour around it. Sometimes that's all it takes to make a losing image a winner.

There is also a more sophisticated analytics option called Iconosquare® that allows you to discover who your top followers are, posting history, best time to post, how people engage with your photos and how many times they come back to them and the growth in your number of followers.

Here are a few more key things to employ to build your audience with your Instagram® account:

1. Identify and cater to your audience. If they have come to expect a certain type of content from you, deliver it!

2. Let your caption tell a story. Just saying, "Here's Fred's before and after," try something like, "Fred was embarrassed by his pimples until he used XYZBrand."

3. Same goes for your pictures. They have to generate a mood, a feeling, a visceral response if they are going to be shared and draw more people to your page. Go for the sensation of being there, so the viewer feels like she's in your shoes — or wants to be.

4. Create a contest. You may find that inviting people to comment, share, or even share their own photo will help followers to engage with your brand.

5. If appropriate, collaborate with another Instagram user by asking them to share their thoughts on your brand. Some may ask for payment, but many will simply ask that you return the favour. This is particularly helpful if you're just getting started and the other person has an established following.

6. Consider advertising on Instagram. According to the media research firm Nielsen, people are nearly 3 times more likely to recall an ad posted on Instagram than normal online advertising.

7. Focus on solid, varied content. Keep your material fresh. Use the filters Instagram offers to enhance, distort or otherwise generate dimension to your visuals.

8. Never hashtag your brand. If you must hashtag, use # before the field your company is in.

What is Twitter®

Like Instagram®, Twitter® is the place where the time-crunched network marketer can make a great impact. Twitter posts are limited to 140 characters — that's characters not words — so you have to remember to say LOL instead of Laugh Out Loud (3 characters instead of 14). While this may seem obvious, the literate introvert may be tempted to use multisyllabic words or phrases. The trick is learning how to be short but sweet — or should I say, "short but tweet"? If your links are too long and eat up too many characters, try bitly.com which helps shorten links.

To get started and officially become a "Tweep," (Twitter user), go to Twitter.com, sign up and build your bio. You'll want to be sure to use an appropriate picture of you, not your product, baby or cat Bruiser. Since you only have 160 characters (ooh, 20 more than a regular "tweet"!) you won't be able to tell your life story. Think Hemingway, not Dickens. Just include things like your company url, something unique about you and what really fires you up. This will likely draw more traffic than where you went to school (unless it's Harvard) or how many kids you have.

Next, start looking for followers. This is simple. Just target people who share your interests and type of business. Then follow the people those people are following. You'll find a pretty high percentage of folks will respond favourably by following you back, particularly if you engage with them by retweeting (sharing something someone else said with your followers) or commenting on their tweets. If someone returns the favour, be sure to thank them. Nothing says connection like gratitude.

Your first Tweet should be something engaging. Include the @ or # symbols before something that interests you to instantly draw a load of people to you. When you use a # it indicates a discussion about something, while the @ symbol is a message meant for a specific person, place or thing. For example, "First tweet. Not sure if @JimmyFallon cares, but I do. Would love to tell him #NBC tour I took. What will #Disneyland be like next week? LOL" Jimmy Fallon might notice your tweet since it was "to" him, and anyone discussing Disneyland and NBC will be able to find you.

If you'd like to take full advantage of Twitter, check out Tweetdeck. Twitter describes this special dashboard thusly, "Create a custom Twitter experience. Organize and build custom timelines, keep track of lists, searches, activity and more — all in one interface. Find exactly what you're looking for. Tweet together. Share an account with your team, without sharing your password. Maintain full control over permissions at all times."[9] You have to see it to appreciate it. You can see as many as nine columns at once, including your followers, @ (to) mentions, Direct Messages (private tweets to friends and associates), and you can even review and post to your Facebook page. Tweet-Deck makes it super easy to keep track of who is retweeting you, so it's easy to express thanks and keep the conversation going.

How to use Twitter as a marketing tool

Whatever you do, don't troll looking for people who have tweeted, "I lost my job." It is far better to use Twitter Lists to find the relevant industries, topics, experts and friends that would appeal to you and make general comment tweets like, "Yeah, if it wasn't for my #residualincome I'd be foreclosed on by now. @JeniferKHood" You really don't have to say anything else. People who are curious will comment or retweet your statement and bring loads more people into your "Twitter-sphere." Just in case you missed it: *Never target an individual with an offer of work or product. This is called trolling and can get you kicked off Twitter and Facebook.*

---

[9] https://support.twitter.com/articles/20169620

If you're looking for leads, it is much better to consistently conduct conversations via Tweetchat.com several times a day, the more the better. Twitter moves much faster than most social media, so actively seek out the #hashtag of the topic you want to be a part of and go for it. You will find that you're doing dozens of tweets a day and getting a load of feedback from folks. So long as you're respectful and interested in someone other than yourself, the folks you're chatting with will become curious about you. Mirror the style of those you follow. Be strategic. If you'd like to meet someone, start to follow that person. Look for conversation starters and jump in. This isn't permission to stalk someone, but it is a way to start a meaningful connection with a prospect who may need what you have. Include links to videos, invitations, and blogs as a way of keeping the engagement between you active.

You may also want to start your own Tweetchat, but be sure you know how they operate by participating in a couple first. You'll be able to gauge whether you want to put in the time and effort to do it productively. If not, don't waste people's time.

Twitter is a terrific vehicle for network marketers because the majority of "Tweeps" are 35-45-year-old entrepreneurs with home-based or small scale businesses. Consequently, you're already hitting your target market and can aim specifically toward the sorts of people who would be most interested in your product. Sell tools? Follow a gal who runs her own contracting business. Sell storage containers? Follow the guy who has a home-based kitchen utensil business.

Not sure who to follow? Twitter has an event made for that. It's called #FollowFriday (aka #FF). Once a week people make posts that include #FF (keeps character count down) and the name of people they recommend following. If you participate in that — which is a wonderful way to build a relationship — be sure to say why the person is a great Tweep to follow. Is she funny? Super talented? Has great links? An expert at something? Just tweet something like, "#FF @introvertednm knows #networkmarketing for #introverts.   Check   out   FB; networkmarketingforintroverts.com."

How effective are Instagram® and Twitter®

Your success with these social media platforms depends a lot on how much time and energy you're willing to put in. If all you can do is post every couple weeks, don't bother. People will not follow you. They want fresh, up to date content. However, if you can put in the requisite amount of time either of these will bring big dividends, as we saw illustrated in the Instagram illustration above.

However, I would recommend choosing one or the other, because if you are really going to participate you very likely only have time for one. If your product is mostly visual, Instagram is a far better choice than Twitter. If your product requires some explanation — and remember the tweets need to be super short — use Twitter.

For example, if your product is a skin care line, you'll want to show before and afters on Instagram; if your product is legal insurance, you'll want to use Twitter. If your product requires a lot of scientific explanation, don't both with either unless you can greatly simplify the information. In which case, obviously, you'll be using Twitter.

Whichever one you use the important thing is consistency, immediacy and mutual give and take.

Chapter 11. Facebook and Your Business

Wow! You're really are popular on Facebook. It must be nice having 1500 friends you've never met. – Unknown

You'd have to be living under a rock to be unfamiliar with Facebook®, but you may never have realized how much of a boon to your business this grand-daddy of all social media can be. For starters, Facebook is the fourth largest *search engine* in the world!

There are a number of things you'll need to know before I get into how to use it as a marketing tool, starting with the fact that Facebook is in almost constant flux, so you should confirm any advice is relevant before using any of the suggestions I make.

The differences in the types of Facebook® Pages

There are Personal pages, Community pages, Business pages and Groups. All but one can be used for business. Can you guess which one? That's right: Personal Pages.

The sole purpose of Personal Facebook pages is to show off the grandkids, pictures from your vacation, share a funny video or an inspirational quote. It is not for your business.

That being said, if you represent a skin care product and someone says, "Gee, Jane, you're looking incredible! Did you get a face lift?" You can answer, "It's that product I told you about." Otherwise, leave it at that or Facebook will pull your page faster than your grandchild can scamper down a hallway!

Community Pages are really designed for church or community groups that share a common cause or interest. These can be used to build interest in subjects related to your product.

Say, for example, your product is related to cooking. You could start a page called, "Salem Area Gourmets," and feature recipes, cooking tips and a link to your business. However, it is best not to directly market with this page as you might lose people before you're ever started. Remember: the essence of successful network marketing for introverts is being able to take it slow and not overwhelm people. A few facts to show you know your stuff will get people curious about you. Then, chances are they'll track you down by checking the website or elsewhere on Facebook.

There is no mistaking Business Pages. There are "Shop Now" buttons, displays of products, prominently displayed logos and ads, the works. Here is where you can be absolutely frank about your need to sponsor, the kinds and types of products you sell and other things related to marketing. However, there are good and bad ways to do so. I'll get to those later along with some other tricks to help turn your Business Page into a cash register.

Finally, there are Groups. These are pages that are for people with shared interests. This may generate some confusion, so here's how Facebook differentiates Groups from the other types of Facebook pages:

PAGES: *Page information and posts information are public and generally available to anyone on Facebook. Anyone can connect with a page and get News Feeds updates. There is no limit to how many people can like a Page. People who manage a page can publish posts as the Page. Page posts can appear in the News Feeds of people who like the Page. Pages can only be created and managed by official representatives.*

GROUPS: *In addition to a public setting, more privacy settings are available for Groups. In secret and closed Groups, posts are only visible to Group members. You can adjust Group privacy to require members to be approved or added by the administrator. When a Group reaches a certain size, some features are limited. The most useful groups tend to be the ones you create with small groups of people you know. In Groups, members receive notifications by default when any member posts in the Group. Group members can participate in chats, upload photos to shared albums, collaborate on Group documents and invite members who are friends to Group events. Groups can be created by anyone.[10]*

---

[10]   https://www.facebook.com/notes/facebook/facebook-tips-whats-the-difference-between-a-facebook-page-and-group/324706977130/

Obviously, there's some legalize tied up with these descriptions, so I recommend keeping it simple. Keep the personal, personal. Keep business, business.

Facebook as a marketing tool

Now that we've gone over the types of pages and ways to keep engagement up, it's time to talk about using Facebook as a marketing device.

There is much to be said for collaboration with your peers. Friends who vouch for your product is the first and probably easiest way to gain some traction. Not only is your list built by attracting their followers to your page, but it gives you that vote of confidence that makes the difference for some people. Just imagine the last time your spouse tried to tell you something but you couldn't hear it. Yet for some reason it's far easier to believe a friend says the same thing. There is something odd about how much we trust those closest to us. Sometimes (not all the time), it makes it hard for us to get our point across.

Your Business, Community and Group pages should have snappy, easy to remember names. Images should rotate regularly. An easy way to do this is think seasons, holidays and activities. In January, your timeline image should be a snowy scene; in July, fireworks and picnics; in November, harvest scenes, etc.

Your smaller image, the one that's usually your face, should be something instantly identifiable and not be changed as often because it's your brand. Some people do things like superimpose hearts around their face in February for Valentine's Day. This generates interest while maintaining the brand. Information should include your website, name, location, and, if appropriate, hours of operation.

This reminds me: never, and I do mean *never*, tell anyone you're going to be out of town in a given week. You'd be surprised how many hateful folks would just love to take advantage of your absence. Instead, post those vacation or convention pictures after you get home.

You will also want to make sure your page is in the right category. Whatever you select should be keyword rich, because that will make it far easier for people to find you.

The "About" area should likewise be chin deep in keywords and exciting descriptors. Having a map, relevant photos, and links to your website and those you like also generates some cross-traffic feeds. So does a thorough work history. People you knew at a job ten years ago may remember you fondly. They may want to reconnect. But if your name is similar to others you'll just blend into the woodwork unless you have something else they can cross-reference with. (I was shocked at how many Jenifer Kay Hoods there are out there.)

The same goes for where you went to school, grew up, interests and even some stuff about your spouse! Now when people find you and like your site, and their friends see your page, there will be instant recognition that this is your "tribe." Remember: the best connections are those with people who know, like and trust you.

Blatant advertising, pitching, and phony pictures of you standing next to a Ferrari are a major buzz kill for former classmates, friends and co-workers. That's why I differentiate between my personal page, my company-related page and my Network Marketing for Introverts page. Nevertheless, plenty of people who know you personally will check out your other Facebook pages and your website just to know more about you, which is why it is so important to create a consistently likable profile.

When I'm ready to launch my group page, I will likewise be circumspect when it comes to coming off too hoity-toity. People have to be able to relate to you. My coach calls this, "showing her panties." By showing your humanity, even in your business page, you can be more effective at connecting. I would never put ads on my personal page because, for one, Facebook would boot me off. More importantly, it lets the cat out of the bag about what I am doing with my life and I know how many people feel about network marketing.

I do put ads and info about my product on my business page, but that's to be expected. However, I try to downplay the effectiveness of my product and just point to evidence, such as before and afters, research or videos. When I do post a video I am careful how I frame it. If it's a rehash of something people may have seen before, I tell people where the new stuff is.

I know I made many mistakes when I first started using Facebook for my business, because I was modelling the way I was taught. I would post these huge rah-rah claims. Engagement was zero. Thank God some people have figured out that's why people get turned off and are helping people do a better job of sharing their excitement.

The book *Network Marketing for Facebook* by Jim Lupkin and Brian Carter has wonderful examples of ways you can help people become engaged with your posts. Here is how they describe an effective versus ineffective post for people representing cleaning products.[11]

---

[11] Lupkin, Jim and Carter, Brian. *Network Marketing for Facebook*. New Ringgold, PA. 2014. 46-47

Most Effective Post

Hey everyone! As you know, I am cautious about what products I use in my home. I found a 100% natural and safe home product line, ranging from cleaning products to clothing detergent.

Would you like a sample?

Less Effective Post

I found an amazing business! You can get all your home products with no chemicals in them. Save your family from the cancer chemicals found in cleaning products! You got to check this out now. I will send you free samples, and you can make money, too, and get rich with me!

Lupkin and Carter rightly point out two things about how these posts are framed. The first one puts the question about samples in its own paragraph, thus increasingly the likelihood it will be read and responded to. The second one sounds like some kind of manic, snake oil style pitch. Remember: too good to be true usually is, so avoid language that will generate skepticism.

Be sure you engage people

Which brings me to a very critical point when it comes to posting on Facebook: The need to engage your followers. It's not enough to have a great "About" page. The effectiveness of your page is limited if people don't read, comment or share your posts.

In fact, no matter how many of the various filters you put on your Facebook page, Facebook determines how many people to show your posts to according to their level of engagement. This is why it is important to stay on top of your pages and keep track of what's working and what isn't.

How many people liked what you posted? How many people shared it? If people are finding your page via friends, chances are engagement levels are up. If you can't think of anything interesting to post, don't bother. It's kind of like putting more water in the soup. Pretty soon there's no flavour. So make sure what you're posting in fun and memorable.

You can figure this out by paying attention to what people are responding to. Last year I posted an old photo of myself when I was a hot, young disco queen. All of a sudden my personal page blew up with people commenting on how I once looked. An old boyfriend shared. Recently I posted a photo of myself on vacation. A few people responded, but no one shared. I guess middle-aged folks are less interesting than sweet young things. Oh well, the point is, it really illustrates the importance of posting stuff that will engage people.

As far as my business goes, I find I have always had a better response when I am showing some third party's information about my product. People trust a theoretically unbiased voice more than a company video. When I do show a company video, I refer people to the part where there is a before and after or a third party testimonial. I say exactly where they will find it. Inspirational quotes also do well.

So ask yourself: "What do my followers most want from me?"

Do they like videos, puzzles, links, humour? Whatever it is, give it to them and the engagement levels will climb, which means Facebook will "show" your page to more people.

By the way, when I say "show" what I am talking about is not only how it shows up in the Newsfeed of people I am already connected with, but also the way Facebook will recommend I connect with someone. A name will pop up on the side or across the top of my Facebook page and say, "Do you know?" or "You may also be interested in." So you can see why engagement is important when it comes to your business.

Now that you know what turns people on, you should have a stash of great quotes, videos, and fascinating supporting documentation on hand for those times when the inspiration is running a little flat. In addition, having a library on hand allows you to can take advantage of Hootsuite or Facebook's own scheduling program to post when you're away or unavailable. But be careful about stepping on people's toes. There's a bunch of stuff that's under copyright, so check morguefile.org for a ready supply of great stuff, and if you're artistic, generate a nice visual to go with it.

But, you ask, how does this help me market my product?

The simplest answer is it begins to create a sense of who you are. It tells people that you're interesting and therefore they "should" participate in your page.

Social Media guru Melissa Galt recommends that your posts utilize some simple techniques to further increase that engagement.[12] They are:

1. **Use a Classic Call to Action** – This is asking people to like, comment or agree with something you've posted.

2. **Give Followers a Choice** – This is posting something that requires an opinion. Yes, or no? This or that? The red one or the green one?

3. **Create a Fun Factor** – This is posting something everyone is sure to love, like a picture of a cuddly puppy.

4. **Make the Picture Worth a 1000 words** – This is making sure the angle, colour or subject of your photo goes a step beyond ordinary and really tells a story. For example, a static photo of someone standing on a beach is far less interesting than a picture of a woman in a bikini strolling toward the ocean with her surfboard under her arm.

5. **Insist on a One Word Response** – This is kind of fun. You say something like, "Using one word only, Batman is the best superhero because he's..." and then see what people say to describe Batman.

---

[12] http://melissagalt.com/

6. **Note Current Events** – This is using something that's going on nationally or locally to engage your followers. It can be something as complex as seeking matching donations or something as easy as expressing support for a person or cause.

7. **Charity Gets Noticed** – If you have an event or fundraiser coming up, make a note of it and ask if anyone is willing to join you in supporting that event. For example, if you will be walking in the next Relay for Life event, ask for sponsors and people to walk with you.

8. **Fan of the Week** – Oo wee! This is outstanding! There's an app on Facebook that allows you to generate a "Fan of the Week." You can show the face of a follower who is super engaged and tell why she's the "Fan of the Week."

9. **Think Outside the Lines** – Don't you hate it when something is just the same old, same old? Like at Thanksgiving there's always the Norman Rockwell painting of the folks about to dig in. Yawn! Try recreating that picture with animals or kids or people who are the antithesis of that wholesome view.

10. **Get Feedback, Ask Questions and Offer Live Coaching** on Facebook – This works best when you ask people to like and share the session. Open the door for people to ask you questions or go to another person's page and give feedback or ask questions there. If your contribution is interesting enough that person's followers might check you out.

11. **Share Your Team** – How do you think your downline would respond if you posted a picture of him standing with you and expressed what makes him a valued member of the team? Likely great, and since he's tagged in your page, his friends will know about it even if he doesn't share.

12. **Show Your Pride and Progress** – Here it is important to not only brag about yourself (in a humble way, of course) but to say why this will help you serve your customers better. For example, "Hey, my upline just told me I'm eligible for a special trip. Wow! Now I'll get a chance to meet with some of the top people in the company and get more training. Does anyone have a question for me to pass along to the higher ups?"

13. **Fill in the Blank** – This is similar to number 5 above, but a little different, in that you're welcoming lengthier responses. The trick is to make your question or statement interesting enough that people will take the trouble to respond. Leave blank lines so people know what they are supposed to respond to.

14. **Ask for a Caption** – This is another fun one. Find an engaging picture and ask for a caption or for someone to suggest what a person might be saying. A picture of someone who looks like they are about to say something are great for this kind of engagement tool, so are before and afters.

15. **Add Emoticons** – It's truly weird, but posts that contain emotions like this one ;=) receive a 52% higher interaction rate than just saying something "wink." Some emoticons get a greater response than others. For example, :D and :P get 2.4X and 2 X higher response rates respectively than a simple smiley.

With engagement comes opportunity to share your product and why you're excited about it. It makes you seem like a fun person to be around. It doesn't require you to be anyone but yourself, but it does require some effort. If you're not willing to make some effort at virtual networking, face-to-face networking will be even harder. This is an awesome way for an introvert to stretch the muscle that likes to have fun and share with people. It also enables introverts to generate lists of the right people, people that will fit in with their sense of humour and interests.

Once you have a decent-sized following and know how to engage the sort of people that fit in with your mindset, you can build your lists by boosting certain posts that are the most likely to draw like-minded people to your page. Boosting can be targeted or general, depending on who you want to reach. I have found that when I boost a particularly uplifting, positive post on my Network Marketing for Introverts Facebook page, and gear it toward an audience of people interested in introversion and MLM, literally hundreds of people respond to my page. I will use keywords like introvert, MLM, home-based business, entrepreneur, networking and spend $5 or $10 and have a huge response. I have sold about 300 copies of my first book by drawing people to my page where they often notice the "Shop Now" button and find their way to Amazon where they can buy it.

Incidentally, the "Shop Now" button may be a no-no with your company, so check it out before employing.

But even if they won't let you use the "Shop Now" button, Facebook also offers instant messaging that allows people to connect with you once they are your "friends." Start by messaging your friends and being personal. Think of what you know about them and how that relates to your product.

For example, your cousin is always running short of cash. "Hi, Tom, I think I may have found a way for you to bring in a little extra every month working with the company I work for. Interested?"

Maybe you have a friend who has complained about food spoilage and you represent Tupperware. "Hey, Jude, I think I may have a solution to lettuce spoiling before you can use it. Would you like me to send you the information?"

If you don't know anyone who needs your product or extra cash (lucky you!), you might just ask for a lead. "Hi, Barb, Listen I've started with a company that sells legal insurance. I know your husband Bob is a lawyer, so you're covered. LOL! But do you know anyone who could use a way to get around the high cost of getting legal advice? Thanks, Mark"

Facebook keeps track of how many people you instant message a day, so keep it at 10 or less. Short little notes like the ones above shouldn't take you more than a minute or two to write, so you can message 10 folks in just 30 minutes or less. Over the course of a month that's 300 people. Some will say yes, some will say no. Don't take anyone's response – or lack of response – personally. Move on and try again in a couple months.

If you do try again, make sure it's not the same message. (Facebook makes it easy to see what you said last time you contacted that person.) "Hey, Jude, I know you said wrapping your lettuce in paper towels was working great for you, but if you'd like to try what I'm using I can lend you my container so you can do a side-by-side test. Interested?" Based on my experiments, I think you will find that about 76% will not respond at all, 4% will say they aren't interested, 12% will respond with a yes or no, and 8% will want the sample. Fortunately, for every ten people I connect deeply with, about two will actually become customers or associates.

Yes, those are terrible odds, but look on the bright side. A huge percentage can be approached again and the small number who say yes will likely be more loyal than someone you pestered into buying your product. Once again, think, "Some will, some won't, so what? Next!" Move on. The law of averages basically confirms that over time those numbers will balance out if you keep building your list. As Kody Bateman notes, "The more people you talk to about your MLM, the less effect shutdowns will have on you."[13]

The thing to keep in mind is the reasons for people not responding can be varied and have nothing whatsoever to do with you personally. They didn't want to hurt your feelings by saying no. They got distracted and forgot about your message. They are on vacation and taking a Facebook break. Who knows?

---

[13] Bateman, Kody. *MLM Blueprint: Your Subconscious Journey to Network Marketing Success*. Salt Lake City, UT. Eagle One Publishing. 2012. 25

Concentrate instead on the people who do become customers. Each of them will likely have an average of 200 friends.[14] If you reach four of those people (2%), that's another 800 potential people who will find their way into your life. People who like products tell their friends about it. This is the essence of network marketing: people who know people who know people. This is why social media is so great, Facebook in particular.

As I mentioned above, there are going to be people who like your pages that you've never met, so writing to them like they are a long lost friend just won't work. A better approach might be to see how they came to follow you. Are they friends with your sister? Then you might respond to a comment they made on your sister's post. This is okay so long as it's germane to what your sister posted.

For example, say your sister has posted something about the rainbow that washed across the sky in front of her house. Her friend Jane says, "Wow! That's gorgeous!" You wouldn't want to respond to that comment with, "Yeah, and it would be even more gorgeous if she washed her windows with X-Brand window cleaner." That's trouble on so many levels. Instead, you'd say, "So true, Jane. Just wish there was a pot of gold at the end of it, eh, sis?" This establishes who you are and how you're all connected. In time, you'll have enough information about Jane to send her an instant message. Until then, you may want to have a special spreadsheet for these sort of "friends."

---

[14] Lupkin, Jim and Carter, Brian. *Network Marketing for Facebook.* New Ringgold, PA. 2014. 56

My Facebook Unknowns

Name	How We're Connected	What Do I Know About
Randall Coffin	Friended me after seeing my post on my brother Dave's FB page	Loves dogs, has a macabre sense of humor, is a helicopter pilot, always broke
Heather Nightingale	Started following me when we were both members of the same coaching group	Nurse, related to Florence, recently traveled to Italy, loves to cook, represents Mary Kay
Tim V. Smith	Not sure. I accepted friend request because liked my NMI page	Introverted, likes most my posts, lives in New Hampshire, maybe he knows or lives near Anne K.
Martha Swearingen	My study buddy with Coaching Group	Doesn't follow up, negative attitude, wishes she could make more money, well-educated

Obviously these are made up names, but you get the gist. The idea is to keep track until they say something I can legitimately connect with. It also helps me know if I even want to bother contacting them at all.

How Often Should You Post?

A good rule of thumb is 80% personal, 20% business related posts. This keep you in front of people without seeming pushy or obnoxious. If you post once a day that would be about 5 personal, 2 business; when you post twice a day, that's 11 personal, 3 business.

To make this easier, look at your company's Facebook page and share a corporate post at least once a day, and write your own post about your business once a day. An example of a personal business post might be:

"I was rough housing with Tyler yesterday and got my favourite jeans all grass stained. If I was still using Blank it would still be there, but I tried my company's detergent and wow! Good as new!"

Another technique would be taking a picture of yourself and asking something relevant about the product. In this case, I'm imagining a jewellery company rep wearing one style earring in one ear and another in the other ear. "I can't decide which of these earrings I want. Which do you think looks best on me?"

In short, making the posts, short, relevant and not overly sales-like will help people engage in a way that's helpful to your goal of generating enough buzz that people start asking about your product. This is also why I recommend no more than two business-related posts per day.

It is far more important to react to your friends' posts, because that's the only way their friends will see your posts. Your "Newsfeed" section has the various posts of your friends, and if you are "friends" with their friends you will see those posts as well. This is part of the incredible exponential power of list building via Facebook. So long as you are respectful and write like a friend and not a salesperson, you will be able to generate real connections with these people regardless of whether you have met them or not. Build credibility, not incredulity.

But I want to be clear: using or manipulating friendships to build your list is not going to help the reputation of network marketing. So, please, be sincere, be authentic and be respectful. This is not an instant solution to your list building needs. Like everything else with network marketing it takes time, patience and consistent effort. Comment or share only when appropriate and relevant to the discussion at hand.

How to Make the Most of Facebook Ads

Buying an ad on Facebook uses tools that are similar to boosting to target your potential audience, yet if you want the best results there are ways to do it that will greatly enhance your chances of success. What follows is a step-by-step guide for winning results.

1. Create a Facebook Fan/Business Page

    a. You cannot buy ads on your personal page

    b. Fan pages get a newsfeed

    c. Fan pages give you metrics to keep track of who is engaged, what engages them and how many people are being reached

2. Create a Facebook Ad Account

    a. Click either the promote button (found right under the Settings tab on the center right of your page) or pull down the menu to the right of the small lock symbol in the blue bar across top of Facebook page (it looks like an upside down triangle) and scroll down to and click "Create Ad"

    b. Determine who your audience is, including selecting keywords to target people who have an interest in your product. Consider age, location, even profession as modifiers. If you have boosted before this may be already set up.

3. Develop an Offer that speaks to your audience

   a. Think of their pain. How can you or your company's product serve them in a way nothing else can?

   b. You only have 90 characters, so be precise and powerful

   c. Text cannot cover more than 20% of any image you use

4. Decide what you're going to link to

   a. A blog, a website, a video or corporate sales page

   b. If linking to a blog or website, you will want to have an autoresponder service such as Aweber or Constant Contact (an email marketing service provider that helps you keep in touch with your subscribers/followers). This will require following some simple instructions to set up a system that captures the contact information of people subscribing to your site.

   c. If you prefer, Facebook has a "Lead Ad Form" in their Publishing tools in the forms library in the back office of a business page (this is where you go to check out notifications, etc.) I prefer an autoresponder myself because I trust it to be unbiased.

d. You should configure it so the autoresponder will confirm the prospect gave you a real email address by offering something in exchange for that person's info. This could be something like a brochure, free sample, coupon, or small booklet. For example, I offer "Six List Building Secrets" to visitors of my Network Marketing for Introverts website.

e. Blogs should also have a capture feature.

5. Decide what you're going to capture

a. I recommend leaving it at first name and email address

b. Some people may also want to add phone numbers, full name and address depending on what they are offering.

6. Make sure you personally respond

a. The autoresponder can be configured to take care of sending things like PDFs and coupons, but if you are sending a free sample, you'll need to respond as soon as the auto-responder sends you a notice saying someone signs up. The message will be something like, "Jane Donut, jdonutsaboutyou@gmail.com, signed up for Network Marketing for Introverts." Needless to say, if you're sending a free sample an address will need to be there, too.

b. A friendly, but not pushy, personal note directly from you saying something like, "Thanks for visiting to my website (visiting my Facebook page, subscribing to my blog). As promised, here is a free sample of XYZ Brand (PDF, coupon). I hope you will find it helpful. If you have any questions, please do not hesitate to call. Meanwhile, if something else comes up that I think you'll find interesting, I'll pass it along."

7. Optional for bloggers — Create a Pixel

a. On the manage ads page there is a Tools menu. You will want to click "Pixels." (not to be confused with pixels in cameras or Pixar cartoons).

b. This will take you to something that will say either Facebook Pixel or Conversion Tracking Pixel (by press time, Facebook may only be offering their pixel). Select one or the other, and then click where it says "Create Pixel."

c. In the Create Pixel page there will be a menu, "Choose the Type of Action You Want to Measure." Scroll down to "Key Page Views" and select that.

d. Name your pixel "Key Page Views – Name of your blog post." This will enable you to keep track of how a particular blog post is doing.

e. You'll get a screen that says, "You have created a Conversion Tracking (Facebook) Pixel." Click on "View Pixel Code" and follow instructions outlined there, starting with copying the code. The directions are slightly more detailed than that so read them carefully and follow those instructions. Honestly, it isn't that complicated if you're moderately tech savvy. Just look for the url in about the middle of the stuff you see on the screen.

f. Go to your website/blog's back office and look for something that says "Head and Footer Code." In WordPress, it is in the Plug-ins under AddFunc. Paste the pixel you copied in Step 7e above where it says, "Head."

g. Go back to Facebook and look at your Pixel. It should say Active under Status (fourth column from left). If it doesn't, you may not have copied and pasted correctly. Try again and if it still doesn't work, contact support.

h. Now create an ad the way we discussed above. When Facebook asks you to "Choose the objective for your campaign," select "Send people to your website."

i. Keep your costs down until you know the ad works for you. $5 a day for a week is only $35, and Facebook will show you just how well you're doing and how much you're spending per engagement in the Manage Ads section of your page. The lower the cost per engagement, the better the ad is doing. You'll find "Manage ads" under the upside down triangle in blue bar at top of Facebook page.

j. Facebook will place your ads in Desktop News Feed, Mobile News Feed, Desktop Right Column and Audience Network. If you want to track where you are getting the most bang for your buck, delete all but one and then run the same ad in another. The same goes for the demographics or other markers you choose to narrow who is looking at an ad. You can even switch out pictures to see if one picture generates more interest than another.

k. You will want to add Google Analytics to your website to keep track of hits at that end as well.

8. Note differences between Facebook marketing options, i.e. Boost, Promote and Ads

   a. Boosting — By far the simplest means of getting more people to look at your Facebook posts. All you do is click Boost (just below Publish button) and you'll be taken to a screen where you can select your target market and how much you want to spend. Cost minimum $2 a day.

   b. Promote — Somewhat more complicated but most of the work is done for you already if you've boosted before. When you choose this option you are promoting your Facebook page. This is great when you have a new business and you want all your friends to see what you have to offer (you can set it up to promote only to people who already follow your personal page), or you can select promoting to a certain demographic that would be a likely customer for the product described on your Facebook business page.

   c. Ads — More complicated because you are advertising the business that is tied to your Facebook page. This could be as simple as generating an ad with your website on it so folks have a way to buy what you're selling. (Being careful to target your market, of course.)

d. Or you can get much more complex and create a pixel that you put on a page of your website so you can track how many people are visiting precisely because they saw the ad on Facebook (or Instagram, Facebook's social media partner) See 7a-k for basics of how to do this more complicated advertising method.

e. In short: Boost posts, Promote Facebook Pages, Advertise Business.

How valuable is Facebook?

Is Facebook worth it? You bet. It's the most recognizable, most universal (over a billion users worldwide), and flexible of all forms of social media. Yeah, it has its quirks. Yeah, it changes policy so often you have to stay on top of it. Yet for sheer reach, nothing can touch it!

Chapter 12. Social Media and Beyond

You are what you share. – Charles Leadbeater

One of the things that's the hardest to grasp about social media is how very public it is.

You say, "Duh!"

I say, "Really. Think about it."

Those pictures of you drunk at your friend's wedding find their way into your teetotaller boss's News Feed. The political opinions you hold and expose may turn some people off. Your comments about someone you know and unfriended may still be seen by a friend of theirs and passed along. Now you see where I am going?

I'm going to go out on a limb here and say that I believe it is best for introverts to be themselves when it comes to social media. But this doesn't mean being disrespectful. It just means being careful about how you express your positions. You don't want to be calling someone stupid. You don't want to be overstating things or exaggerating. Socially – in person, that is – introverts generally know this intuitively. But when it comes to the anonymity of social media, it is easy to let our inner tiger come out because we tend to hide behind words.

While extroverts find it much easier to share their feelings and opinions in a crowd of strangers, introverts are likely to congregate primarily with people who share their interests and likes. I know my face contorts when I am confronted by someone who says something I consider inane. How about yours? If you're like me, you feel best when you're with people who understand you. That's why I choose to be a careful version of myself when posting on social media.

Dos and Don'ts

Be yourself. Be as kind as you can be. Listen carefully. Don't argue. Reflect what you heard, and upon confirmation that you have it right — and only if it seems appropriate — counter respectfully.

As stated in my previous book, the most important skill in communication is listening. This requires giving people time to fully express an idea or opinion. If we do not listen carefully and compassionately, we're likely to hear things that aren't there, or only partially there. This usually reflects a defensive rather than an open-hearted interpretation of what the person said. For example:

Prospect: I've heard that lead is bad for you and that's why I am not going to buy your cast iron pans.
NM: So you're saying you're not going to buy from me.

The real issue for this prospect is his fear that there is a toxic substance like lead in your cast iron pans. You can guide the conversation better by reflecting back what the person said, getting confirmation and then gently countering without making the person wrong about the toxic nature of lead. Instead you affirm his concern and educate him about your product.

NM: If I understand you correctly, you're worried about lead being in our pans. Is that right?

Prospect: Yes.

NM: You're right to be concerned about lead. I would be too. Fortunately, any lead in cast iron melts away before the pan is cast, sort of like the alcohol in wine is cooked away when the wine sauce reaches a certain temperature.

You may also run into arguments about network marketing being a pyramid scheme. Tell yourself every time you're speaking with someone: Don't Argue, Just Listen, Reflect, Confirm, and Counter. If you tell yourself this again and again it will retrain your brain and become a profitable habit!

Here are a few good counters to that common misconception about our industry.

"The only difference between my commission and the person above me is she has more people on her team than I do. As far as per sale goes, we are paid the same."

"That's funny, because well-known financial experts like Warren Buffet say it's the best kept secret in the business world."

"I think things have come a long way since the old days. These days it's a $100-Billion-dollar industry where anyone can make money."

"Have you read, *In Search of Excellence*? The author, Tom Peters, calls network marketing the first truly revolutionary shift in marketing in the last 50 years. Maybe that's because he believes leaders don't create followers. Leaders create more leaders."[15]

"The question isn't why do the top 5% make more money than I do? The question is what can I do to earn that much myself. It's like the old story of the gal who goes from the mail room to the board room. She had to work her butt off. She had to have a positive, can-do attitude. That's what I'm going to do."

"I have found it's just like any business. You make what you put into it. I know I'm getting commission and I suspect you can, too."

This is the fine line network marketing requires. Express yourself while always imagining who may be listening. I know I have blown it many times with my personal page, but my business pages are just that — Business with a capital B. In hindsight, I wish I'd been more careful with my personal page, too. But since that's water under the bridge, I have trained myself to be more circumspect. As a result, my followers have grown.

---

[15] https://www.entrepreneur.com/article/84228

Do be informative. Do be casual. Do use loads of visuals, surveys, personality tests, and other things to engage people. Make people laugh. Stay positive. Be creative and fun. Support your team and company in every way you honestly can.

Don't argue, besmirch, use foul language, attempt to steal someone else's lead, criticize another product or company or make unsubstantiated claims. All these will be the death of your business and, in another sense, the death of any casual friendships you have.

When the Private You Meets the Public

While your true friends understand your need to occasionally blow off steam with nasty remarks, sarcasm and foul language, the rest of society and the social media universe might not be so forgiving.

There will be times when, in spite of your best efforts, your less attractive sides come through. As quickly as possible, forgive yourself, apologize and move on. Letting something you said in the heat of the moment linger only makes it stink more.

This is one reason why I stress the importance of acting like an introvert if you are one. Whenever I try to be an extrovert just to please someone I find I am obnoxious because I am forced to turn off the part of myself that makes me, me. I suspect many of you have had the same experience.

The extrovert says, "Come on! Don't be such a stick in the mud." You go out dancing even if you're a lousy dancer. You use "Dutch" courage to try and loosen up and your tongue starts to wag. You get as loud as the extroverts in the room but you don't have the extrovert's natural joie de vivre and suddenly people wonder why you're even there. Believe me, I've seen it and lived it. So honour your personality type by being the person others feel they can confide in. Be true to yourself by speaking when something interests you, not because it's expected. Be real about your limitations, but be willing to stretch past the ruts in your life.

You Still Need Personal Contact

Just because you're having a load of fun online doesn't mean you don't have to personally connect with people. This is by far the hardest part of network marketing for an introvert.

Leave the house. Woo boy! I can see a lot of you sweating at that suggestion, but honestly, we must if we want our business to grow. Find a safe place to hang out, such as a club, library, coffee shop or other place where you'll find your tribe and allow yourself the pleasure of connecting with someone. You can choose to expand your circle to include people who share your interests and hobbies.

For example, if you're a birdwatcher, how hard can it be to go someplace where people are birdwatching and sidle up to someone and say, "I thought I saw a white-winged crossbill in that spruce over there, but I've never seen one this far west. Did you see it?" You will instantly have a person interested in your fascination in this rarely sighted bird. If you let the friendship bloom naturally (that is, don't tackle him with your product two minutes later), you will eventually be able to discuss what you do and why.

In my first book, I went over a load of tips for how to go from being a wallflower to a social butterfly.[16] I understand techniques like these may require you to stretch outside your comfort zone, but if you're serious about being a successful network marketing professional, steps like this are necessary.

As I discussed in Chapter 9, using Meetup® is a great way to find people who will fit easily into your world.

Going to Toastmasters will also help you gain confidence for speaking to strangers. A supportive group of people who struggle with being articulate is not only a great way to improve your speaking skills, but is also a wonderful place to safely present your product and connect with people.

---

[16] Hood, Jenifer Kay. *Network Marketing for Introverts: A Relationship Guide for the Shy, Timid and Reserved.* Salem, OR. Cyrano Publishing. 2015. 62-69

By the way, don't make every Toastmasters speech or Meetup® about your product. Share some elements of your life story and your interests. Believe me, people are more receptive when you talk about your product if they know, like and trust you.

I also suggest asking friends to introduce you to their friends in a casual way. Usually one's work or church friends don't know one's personal friends. Try asking a church friend to introduce you to people she knows in the area outside church. She may ask why and you can say, "I'm just trying to challenge myself to be more social. I thought since you and I already have so much in common that your friends would also share interests. Since I'm an introvert, I'm hoping broaden my circle in a way that feels safe for me."

Your main objective is meeting more people, not pitching them. This way you'll be likely to find people with at least some similar interests and values when you socialize. Those are the type of folks you will want to work with.

Similarly, if you're just starting your business, you can have a launch party and invite all your friends and family. This is your opportunity to explain to them what you're doing and why and ask for their help getting started. Do not insist they all sign up as your downlines or customers. Rather, just offer those options and the easier path of pledging to help you connect with more people. Help them understand this is a numbers game. Promise to be respectful and not to jeopardize friendships.

If you have done a good enough job explaining what your product is and why you chose the company and industry, chances are they will be less prone to blow you off. If they do try to discourage you, politely say you've already looked into those objections and want to give network marketing a try anyway. (See suggested come backs to criticism about the industry above.)

From Victim to Victor

Successful people are always learning. They are ready to open their minds and change their modus operandi if it benefits them. It is particularly important in this industry to change your paradigm from victim to victor.

Over the course of my three years in the industry, I have devoured self-help books like crazy. Yet I still felt I needed some one-on-one help and support. I looked around, took advantage of some of the many free courses out there and found one I resonated with. After viewing her material, I thought it might be worth it to hire her as my coach. I reasoned that if I was truly serious about my business, I had better take this opportunity to have someone help me see what the missing link in my business was.

The sort of coach that works for one person will not necessarily work for another. I used to watch *The Biggest Loser*. I often mused that Bob Harper would be a better coach for me than Gillian Michaels. There is nothing wrong with either approach. I just know myself well enough to know that I would have rebelled against Gillian's screaming tough love. Fortunately, I've never been so overweight that I needed that sort of help, but if I did, I knew I would look for someone who knew how to motivate me and be tough without ticking me off.

Think about what sort of coaching you like. If you aren't athletic (and most introverts aren't), think of a favourite teacher or counsellor. What was it about that person that you resonated with?

Once you've identified the best sort of coach for you, go and find him or her. I strongly advise this be someone outside your company. Sure, it's wonderful to have people familiar with your product to bounce things off of, but what I am talking about is someone who is more likely to be objective. Too many uplines tend to subconsciously push you in ways that will help them make money, but will do little to help you get over whatever it is that's hanging you up inside.

An independent coach can look at what you're doing and guide you toward thinking and acting differently. If you have an issue with money, seek a money coach. If you have an issue with self-esteem, seek a counsellor or a coach who is motivational. If you struggle with staying positive, find someone who can help you look at the bright side without being so Pollyanna that you can't stomach their advice. Obviously, if you have any mental health problems you need to see someone qualified to help you with that. Otherwise, a coach who can address your weaknesses will help lift you toward success.

I needed to think differently about my life, particularly my relationship with money. So I found someone who could help me make this paradigm shift. We have twice monthly one-on-one calls, twice monthly group calls and loads of webinars, as well as a bunch of social media based support.

The side benefit of my choice is my coach allows me to connect with her other clients, most of whom are struggling with the same issues. This allows me to share my troubles and my business while getting advice from others about what is and isn't working as I talk about my product. These folks have no vested interest in me making a sale. Their unbiased, freely spoken, but respectful, comments have helped me identify the weaknesses in my approach. Some members have even purchased products from me.

As an introvert you may find certain things more challenging than others. Any weak link can be maneuvered around so long as you're willing to admit it. It takes a lot of courage to measure where you are and do something about it. If you aren't able to muster consistent dedication, strong self-esteem and compassionate listening, there's no shame in asking for help. Just do it and watch your business grow!

> **EXTROVERTS TAKE NOTE:** If your introverted downline is not responding to you, it isn't because she doesn't appreciate your help. It's either because you're pushing too hard or in a way that rubs her the wrong way, such as suggesting she act like an extrovert. Relax. Let her know you're available if she needs help. Then back off. If you don't understand why an introvert would act this way, read Susan Cain's book, *Quiet*.

Chapter 13. Hidden Avenues for List Building

When you talk to people, share what you are. Stop focusing on all the things you aren't. Focus on your abilities and the talents you do have. Then just smile. You'll be amazed at what it does for them and for you!

— *Dan Pearce*

Without a doubt, having a solid list is essential to your network marketing business. We've already discussed many ways you can use social media to build your list, taking classes, joining groups, and asking friends for leads. Here are a couple more ways to expand your list that weren't found in my first book.

Take a trip down Memory Lane and bring to mind folks who are adventurous, fun, smart, and hardworking. In a spreadsheet like excel or in a notebook, make columns for their names, how you know them, and everything you know about them. This would be something similar to what I illustrated above in the chapter about Facebook when I discussed connecting with friends of friends, only it will list where these former classmates, work buddies or neighbors are from, where they grew up, what they do for a living, schools attended and majors, etc. Now make a column for a moment you shared that really addresses the kind of connection you have. If you're not sure how to do this, simply imagine how they would respond if they heard from you. Is it likely they will remember something you did together?

Now, with that picture in mind, try finding them via Facebook®, LinkedIn®, Google®, etc. and contact them with a hearty, "Hey, I was thinking about that time we went to the conference together and started singing in the elevator. It cracked me up and got me curious. What are you up to these days?" This is a painless way to reopen dialogue with someone who might be a great team member.

This person will have had a real connection with you at some point, so the lead is at least tepid, maybe even very warm. I've had extroverted uplines tell me to contact everyone in my high school graduating class and mention a teacher. To my way of thinking, nothing smacks of desperate more than, "Hi, you used to throw spitballs at me in Mrs. Simpson's English class at Blair and I'm just wondering if you've matured enough to go into business with me." Doesn't it make more sense to contact an old study buddy and talk about something real and positive that happened between you?

There are literally hundreds of people I have had some kind of contact with who would be willing to reconnect with me. So long as I don't tackle them with my product in the first moments of re-establishing contact, I will soon have access to them, their family, their friends and their co-workers via personal and social media contact. Network marketing is all about establishing (or re-establishing) a connection with someone and sharing a wonderful product or opportunity. People are grateful when the friends they know, like and trust help them out. People are suspicious and hostile when someone contacts them out of the blue just to tell them about a product they are selling. While it may take longer to go through "select" people as opposed to "random" people, the chances of stable success are far higher.

The industry is rife with stories of people who built a huge team and then it all fell apart at the first sign of economic instability. My guess is a good percentage of those folks who scurry away are people who have no vested interest in helping a friend succeed. Of the people I have sponsored using the methods recommended by extroverted uplines, *not one* has stayed with me longer than one year. The true friends I have sponsored have been with me through thick and thin. When they lost a job or had some event that stretched them, they have postponed their autoship, not cancelled it.

The trick is being able to develop a list with enough vested interest to make it through the bad times. This kind of genuine camaraderie will also encourage customers to offer leads even if they have no interest in the business themselves.

I would argue that building a stable team is more important for introverts than building a huge but uncommitted team. Introverts tend to be sensitive to people dropping out. If too many people drop out all at once, a sense of futility is much more likely to overtake you — unless you've developed a super strong "MLM Blueprint." You have two main responsibilities as a network marketer:

1) Build your team as stable, wide and deep as you can;

2) Work on your tolerance for rebuilding your team because it will be necessary every now and then.

A few simple tricks to build your email list

I have already spoken of how one can direct traffic to a website using Facebook with an autoresponder service like Aweber, Constant Contact, Mail Chimp or Infusionsoft that will capture names and addresses. This takes some set up time, but is well worth it. Using this method, I was able to add over 100 names to my list in three months, which is almost a lead a day.

No website? Or your company only allows you to use their website for business? Here's a solution that most likely your company won't have any problem with — though I'd check, just to be sure. Check out Leadpages.com and use their simple but effective templates to generate a landing page in 15 minutes or less. The landing page you build is sort of like a webpage, only the content is limited to one page and its sole function is generating interest. With a powerful headline and well-worded call-to-action, combined with one of the great visuals already built into their templates, you can entice viewers to give you their name and email address in exchange for something that they'll find worthwhile using the same autoresponder tool I described in the Facebook® chapter.

What you offer may not even be product. It can be something related to your product. For example, say you represent a legal insurance company. You could offer a short booklet called, "Eight Simple Estate Planning Steps." Chances are this will hit your target market of older folks who are considering such things and have investments they want to protect. Similarly, you could offer, "Ten Steps to Protect Yourself from Identity Theft." The key here is thinking of your target market and coming up with something that would definitely turn them on and get them to make that exchange.

You can even mix it up by exchanging weekly tips for someone's name and email address. This won't work for everyone, but for some industries it will be fabulous. For example, if you represent a health and fitness company, you could compile a nice long list of healthy recipes and then offer "Weekly healthy recipes" to your subscribers.

After building your landing page and setting it up with an autoresponder, promote it everywhere you can. Use all forms of social media, word of mouth, flyers and direct mail. You can mention the page at a talk or meeting you attend. Add it to your LinkedIn® page, your bio or blog. In short, make sure it is everywhere your target market might see it.

Once you have established this relationship, the chances are far greater the subscriber will open up your email when you send them an invitation to visit your business (company) website or attend a meeting with you personally somewhere. This doesn't mean you have to become a public speaker; you just have to drive traffic to one of the many group meetings your company is probably having in your area. Ask an extroverted upline to host the meeting and do the presenting.

This kind of secondary outreach is a type of content upgrade. You've given them recipes for a month or so. Next, they receive an email from you that says, "You want to take your health to the next level? Join me on Thursday at the Salem Public Library for a talk on, "How Diet and Emotional Well-being Are Linked." In other words, you're offering them something to take them to the next level beyond your free recipes and it's also free. Yes, the cynical will blow it off, but the serious will jump at the chance to check out what you have to offer.

> EXTROVERTS TAKE NOTE: Be sure to announce all local meetings well in advance so your introverted downline can use social media to drive traffic to the event. While he should also be personally inviting folks to events like this, social media is likely to generate many more folks than traditional face-to-face invitations.

Taking the above to the next level

What if there was a way to add an even larger pool of targeted prospects in a relatively short amount of time?

There is: and it piggybacks on the method we just went over. It's called a Joint Venture (JV) Giveaway.

If you're willing to put in a few hours a week toward this goal and offer an inducement, a joint venture giveaway is a relatively simple technique to help you build your business by building your list.

With this method, a group of business owners who offer complimentary services and who share a common target market, join forces and 'give away' a small but desirable freebie or discount such as described above. For example, say you represent a fitness company. You would seek out partners in other industries that are related to health and fitness. This could be non-competitors specializing in massage, diet, skin care and other body products. The partners can be all over the map or local vendors. Each would offer something to visitors to the "Event" page for a certain time period.

A JV Giveaway requires some groundwork, but it's well worth it. One person takes the lead in organizing the event and creates an "Event" landing page. This page can either be a Facebook business page or a landing page akin to what I have described above. In both cases, all participants will have to have an autoresponder account and a place to direct people to claim their free gift or discount.

If you're using a landing page, make sure you have all the information from the participants and expenses (if any) covered before you publish the page. If there are expenses, I recommend either splitting the costs equally among participants, or putting the folks who contribute to the cost at the top of the page.

In the case of Facebook, you'll have to find a way of splitting the cost of the ad buy or page promotion. Perhaps you all mutually agree that you will spend $20 a day on the ad or promotion and run the event for 10 days. This will cost the group $200. So if you have ten participants each participant must send $20 along with their blurb about what they are giving away and a link to it before they will be posted in the ad. Do not allow anyone to be exempt from paying. If you do, you risk resentment among the other participants. Facebook has a sort of scrolling ad that could show each person's offering in a randomized manner. If the group prefers, each person will post their giveaway themselves after they have paid their share. You, as administrator, can use Page setup to limit who can post on your page.

All partners then promote the event to their individual lists and networks via email. These prospects are directed to the event page where the visitor will see a selection of free giveaways linked directly to the websites of the JV partners. If they want the gift, they click the link. As stated above, you don't need a full on website for this sort of exchange; a landing page will do.

To understand how effective this strategy is, let's take a look at the numbers. If you collaborate with nine other joint venture partners, and all ten of you have a prospect list of 300 warm leads, that's a potential target audience of 3,000. If your free gift is enticing enough, you may get nine new leads for every one of the names on your list. As you can see, it helps you make an exponential leap in the number of people you're reaching. The important thing to remember is not to use this expanded list as permission to start spamming. Your JV Partners will not be happy as it will reflect on them. Consequently, they'd be much less likely to send future referrals!

If you don't want to go to the trouble of a JV Giveaway, you can simply find some strategic partners and exchange lists. This requires a little finesse, but it can be done. Mark has a friend named Cheryl whose business complements his. He sends a short email to all his contacts (or prearranged number of contacts) saying, "Hi! I want to turn you on to my friend Cheryl. She's just started a new business and is giving away discount coupons. If you know anyone who could use this help, please check out Cheryl's website and claim your coupon." Then Cheryl does the same for Mark. "Hi, my old friend Mark recently turned me on to the most amazing natural cleaning products I've ever used. You know how important doing things naturally is to me and this stuff really works. He's offering a super discount on the amazing detergent his company makes. Here's link to Mark's site in case you want to try it out."

Don't like online? Go offline

Texting is an increasingly popular method of reaching out to people, and text messaging tools like Leaddigit, Salesforce and Eztexting, can substantially increase your list without ever going online.

In you don't already have a smart phone, get one. In our increasingly mobile world, you can't afford not to have this "Swiss Army Knife" of communication. Not only will it let you make calls on the fly and take pictures, but it will also let you take an order or sign up an excited prospect before they cool down. Smart phones also have calendars, calculators, flashlights, and the ability to go online to Google something, show a video, or check email no matter where you are!

If this isn't enough, you can use it to build your list in real time. Here's how:

1. Download a text messaging tool that suits you best (some of them are listed above, but there are many others).

2. Ask potential leads to text a certain word or phrase to the short phone number you've generated using the text messaging tool. For example, say you have long or complicated website. You could say, "My website address is a real bear, but if you text the word "website" to 12345 you'll get a direct link sent to your phone."

3. When they do so, the tool immediately sends a text reply with something like, "Thanks for the text. Here's the link you requested."

4. You now have their phone number. You can make this a "two-fer" by having an autoresponder generated goodie when they get to your website or landing page that captures their name and email address. Voila! Instant lead generation.

There are numerous ways to introduce this method to a prospect.

1. You can add it to a social media page post or bio.

2. You can add it to your business card.

3. You can mention it when meeting someone and you don't want to take too much of their time.

4. You can use it with a giveaway and on a Facebook ad.
5. You can include it on a flyer.
6. You can share it during a presentation

Whatever you offer must have value and not just be junk. A well-designed call to action that clearly explains what the prospect is going to get, explained in a way that addresses *their need*, not yours, will generate a lot of positive attention and shares.

How to Accelerate with People

Never underestimate the power of an experienced network marketer. If you hear of someone who is a successful entrepreneur looking for a new MLM company, immediately contact that person and share your opportunity.

An upline of mine, a true extrovert, recently said that the fastest way toward momentum is sponsoring a lot of people fast. For an extrovert this might be relatively easy, but for an introvert this is somewhat unrealistic unless you're capable of sublimating your need for quiet time long enough to connect with 100 new people a week.

Some of the techniques we've discussed so far, such as the Joint Venture Giveaway, can help you connect with that many people. Nevertheless, you still have to call them, follow-up and sign up enough people to average two new customers or associates a week if you want to build fast. For an introvert, this kind of intensive outreach may be asking too much, but it is not impossible if you're willing to consider the challenge a kind of sprint to this finish of a long marathon.

On the other hand, I believe if you make 8-10 calls a day, and half of those are to people who rejected you a short time before, you will build a team. Sure, you won't win any prizes for speedy team building, but that's not what you're about anyway, is it? You don't need to get a prize to know you're doing your best. It might be nice but it isn't the "be all and end all." You're just happy to see consistent progress. At least, I am. A customer or associate a month is reasonable for me. I know this will mean a longer slog until I have a big enough team to make huge money, but it will be a strong team that is more capable of withstanding shifts in the economic winds.

Nonetheless, that extroverted upline's point is well-taken. The faster you build, the more you make, and what better way to build than finding as many Dedicated, Hardworking and Experienced network marketers as you can. These DHEs, as I call them, are my Holy Grail, and I actively seek them out. I have found when I sign someone with little or no experience they will drop out unless they have a strong connection to me or an affinity for my products. Signing DHEs just makes sense.

DHEs will reach out to their existing lists to draw people in. Members of their old teams will become members of their new teams, and by extension your team. So seek out the DHEs. Ask friends if they know anyone who is a DHE. Look for them in booths at local events and take their card. While attempting to recruit them through their social media pages is considered bad form, you can approach people face-to-face if they post their number on cork boards or the decal on their cars.

When approaching a DHE simply ask if they are happy where they are or if they are looking for a new challenge. If they are, make sure you treat them like royalty. Check in with your upline and do a three-way call with them. See if they are qualified for special treatment or a visit to corporate headquarters. Do whatever it takes to impress upon that person that you value them and they will be welcomed in your company. The numbers they will bring to you will be worth every uncomfortable moment, I guarantee you!

Besides, some companies even allow you to represent more than one company so long as you're not competing. You might be able to sell legal insurance and kitchen ware and thereby, in effect, double your list right there. Likewise, the DHE you approach from a non-competing company might welcome the chance to earn a little more by having two businesses and be willing to work for you.

The importance of follow-up

As an introverted network marketer you may overlook or sidestep an important step while you are busy list building: If you've made a connection with someone, be sure to follow up. Not calling a second, third, or even fourth time, is like dropping money on the ground and not picking it up. And don't worry, introverts! If you've made a connection — and have permission to email, text or call the person — it won't matter how many times you contact them so long as you don't make a pest of yourself. Just be sure to make your message relevant and unique each time you connect. It once took me eight calls to finally reach someone who called me back because he admired my persistence.

Chapter 14: How to Train Your Extrovert

As long as you model others, you will only be a copycat, but you will never be the best copycat in the world. But you will be the best you that you can be if you define your value to the world. Someone's opinion of you doesn't have to become your reality. ~ *Will Smith*

In my previous book, I had a chapter designed for extroverts. I hoped it would give them the tools to be more compassionate and understanding of their introverted team mate's style.

In this book, I'd like to suggest that you take the bull by the horns and train your extroverted uplines in the best way to work with you. Why? Because a well-trained extrovert can be an introvert's best friend and ally.

This starts with having a nice sit down chat and asking the extrovert to just hear you out. It will help you stay on track if you have a list of what you need to cover and, depending on the person, help the extrovert track what you're saying.

What follows are a few things your extrovert needs to know right out of the gate.

1. Introversion is neither a pathological or abnormal condition.

2. Introverts comprise between 35-50% of the total population (most modern studies lean toward the latter figure).

3. Introverts may be the minority, but they are a majority in the gifted population (Gallagher, 1990; Hoehn & Birely, 1988).

4. Introverts get their energy internally and find social interaction draining.

5. The introvert's main focus is the internal world of ideas and concepts (the mind); the extrovert is primarily concerned with the external world of people and activities (Myers & Myers, 1980). Tell your extrovert that you usually live inside your inner world and rarely let others into it, which may lead him or her to make erroneous decisions about you and your needs. For example, if you are quiet, it doesn't necessarily mean you're sad or angry. You just may be processing something.

6. Tell your extrovert it is *not* his or her job to try to help you become more social, verbal, and outgoing. This generally has the opposite effect. When pushed, you will become even more drained, taciturn, and withdrawn. Ask him to make it okay to be yourself.

7. While you may appear outgoing, it is only a mask you wear to survive in an extrovert-centric world. In fact, studies show that introverts fall into two distinct categories:

   a) **Group A** [the one often mistakenly thought of as extroverted, e.g. this would be someone like the author of this book]: Self-sufficient, confident, hardworking, with firm goals, self-actualizing, reserved, preferring activities that involve inner experience and introspection; and

b) **Group B:** Shy, timid, withdrawn with low self-concept, lacking in communication skills, demonstrating fear of people, dread of doing things in front of others, preference for being left alone.

8. Sometimes you will display the qualities mentioned in Group B as the consequence of frequent criticism for not being more social or outgoing. [17]

The Introvert and the Extrovert: Oil and Vinegar Can Make Salad Dressing

Once you've acquainted your extrovert with these facts, it's time to move on to how you both can work within your different styles. Start by establishing a secret word between you that tells the extrovert to back off.

It may sound like something kinky, but it's not. It's self-preservation. If the extrovert wants to get the best out of you, and you want to give the situation your best, you have to be able to withdraw when you're tired and overstimulated. Help your extrovert understand that you operate best under pre-set conditions and that you will do your part to stretch as far as you can to work with the team. Here are some things you might want to explain.

1. You like to arrive early so you're not overwhelmed by walking into a room full of strangers.

---

[17] *Education*, 2001, Vol. 101:1:39

2. Let your extrovert know that it is better for him or her to have an introvert-friendly task for you to do at events. It gives you control over the situation

3. You prefer tasks that do not require you to be front and center.

4. If you are ready to leave the event, you can say the code word to your extrovert. In exchange, you promise you will always check in with yourself and go out of your comfort zone as much as possible before telling him or her you're leaving.

5. Ask your extrovert to back you up when other people want you to stay, but you have signalled your desire to leave.

6. Tell your extrovert that you do not like to be pushed to speak. Asking once or twice is enough. Beyond that he or she is just being annoying and you'll clam up even more or make an ass of yourself.

7. Ask your extrovert to try to avoid interrupting you when you do speak up because it will shut you down.

8. You will consciously try to situate yourself in environments that are suitable to your personality.

9. You will organize your life in terms of what personality psychologists call ultimate levels of arousal and what Susan Cain calls 'sweet spots,' and by doing so feel more energetic and alive than before.[18]

---

[18] Cain, Susan. *Quiet: The Power of Introverts in a World That Can't Stop Talking*, New York: Broadway Books. 2013. 124-125.

10. You will do whatever you can to sustain your "sweet spot" by having the courage to ask for advance notice of speaking engagements, preparing what you are going to say ahead of time, and asking for the quiet space you need to work productively and recharge your batteries.

11. Ask your extroverted friend to be your "wing man" in case you're caught in an effort to find the right words. With his or her compassion and your preparation, you will be far more at ease.

12. Tell your extrovert it will be easier for you if things are not sprung on you at the last minute. You prefer to plan ahead because it helps you stay focussed.

13. Let your extrovert know that what they did to get over a fear may not work for you. Likewise, what they did to build a list may be next to impossible for you.

14. Promise to work on stretching yourself in whatever way you can. Let your extrovert know you're aware of what it takes to have success in network marketing and you are educating yourself and doing all you can to find ways to build your list, make contacts, educate, network and follow-up.

15. Say you will take part in all meetings you can, study any material he or she suggests, work on self-esteem issues, get the help you need through team mates, courses and coaches.

16. Explain how the best way to be helpful is to make use of your natural gift for research and study, not suggest something that works for extroverts. For example, instead of suggesting you go door to door with fliers, the extrovert might ask if you've read Eric Worre's memory jogger. This will support you in a way that is in sync with your personality and allows you to build your marketing muscles gradually by guiding you toward lukewarm rather than cold leads. Remember: one cannot run until one first walks. If your extrovert lets you acclimate, eventually your fear will dwindle to a manageable size.

> EXTROVERTS TAKE NOTE: Listening and absorbing what your introvert needs from you is the best investment you can make for building a stable team.

17. Tell you extrovert your why (the reason why you are choosing to build a network marketing business) and ask him or her to give you the tools to address it. Some whys are about more than making money. Some whys are about time with the family. For example, dragging you to an event when it's your daughter's graduation is only going to build resentment.

18. Your extrovert should be given permission to be serious when he or she needs to. Promise to offer that space, with the understanding the favour will be returned.

19. Tell your extrovert, "Please don't attempt to soothe, attempt to understand." Soothing tends to feel dismissive. Use the kind of communication skills Steve Shapiro talks about in *Listening for Success* to understand at a deeper level.

20. Ask your extrovert to reward you in a way that's meaningful for you. The usual awards and shout outs announcing your achievements may not be as effective as a handwritten note acknowledging your accomplishment and cheering you on to the next.

21. Teach your extrovert that you may need to work at a different pace than he or she does. So long as you are making consistent effort, that should be enough for your extrovert.

22. Tell your extrovert, "Don't say I'm uncoachable." Effective coaches know the strength and weaknesses of their team members. Asking you to stretch is one thing. Asking you to change is another.

23. Ask your extrovert to stop thinking about introversion as something that can be fixed. Tell him or her to think of it as a different style of social interaction. While at times you may act like an extrovert, he or she shouldn't assume it's easy for you. That surface impression masks intense discomfort and emotional stress.

24. Promise to do your best to enter into a personal "Free Trait Agreement." This will allow you to play the role of extrovert as often as you feel comfortable doing so.

25. Request that your extrovert balance his or her training methods to make sure you and the other introverts in the room feel comfortable and understand what is expected. Remind them that introverts prefer independence and need plenty of downtime to absorb what they've learned.

Where to Draw the Line

Making an effort to find common ground and work out solutions will help you build a more sustainable and successful team.

Studies have shown that introverted leaders are 20 percent more likely to follow suggestions and 24 percent more likely to build teams with better results.[19] When downlines are empowered to take initiative, their teams outperform those led by extroverts by 14 percent. [20] Teams view introverted leaders as more approachable and receptive to ideas, which motivates the team to work harder.

> Because of their inclination to listen to others and lack of interest in dominating social situations, introverts are more likely to hear and implement suggestions. Having benefited from the talents of their followers, they are likely to motivate them to be even more proactive. …Employees who take advantage of opportunities in a fast-moving, 24/7 business environment without waiting for a leader to tell them what to do, are increasingly vital to organizational success. To understand how to maximize these employee's contributions is an important tool for all leaders. It's also important for

---

[19] Cain, Susan. *Quiet: The Power of Introverts in a World That Can't Stop Talking*, New York: Broadway Books. 2013. 57

[20] Ibid. 56

companies to groom listeners as well as talkers for leadership roles.[21]

If your extrovert starts trying to push you toward being or doing something you don't want to do, stand up for yourself and say, "No." Remind your extroverted team member that introverts have the persistence, listening skills, and self-reliance that any busy leader would want on her side. They stabilize teams, are aware of challenges ahead of time, and work with less ego and more team spirit. In short, you have every right to stand up for yourself because it's worth your upline's effort to adjust to the introverted personality style.

---

[21] Cain, Susan. *Quiet: The Power of Introverts in a World That Can't Stop Talking*, New York: Broadway Books. 2013. 57-58

Chapter 15. Final Thoughts for NMI 2.0

Start by doing what is necessary, then do what's possible, and suddenly you are doing the impossible.
— St Francis of Assisi

Network marketing guru M. J. Durkin believes there are three types of entrepreneurs: Farmers, Sharecroppers, and Hunters. Some of us fall into one category more naturally than another. Each type has value. The Farmer plants the seeds and nurtures the relationships. The Sharecropper takes the leads others give him or her and runs with them. When the seeds he plants are passed along, he pays for the use of the "land." Hunters are always on the prowl for "food" that will feed their team. I would like to spin these a little and spend a minute discussing the importance of incorporating at least some aspect of all three in your business as an introverted network marketer.

Every lead you get requires you to water it with gentle, respectful and ethical communication. If you take advantage of your upline's extroversion, offer some recognition of their assistance in helping you harvest the "crops." If you do not hunt for leads somewhere you will go hungry.

What tools will you need to "bring in the sheaves"

I have already mentioned signing up for an autoresponder service, using a cell phone, a texting service, building landing (or web) pages, and social media to develop your lead base. Here are a few other tools you should have:

1. A calendar service — This allows your prospects to set up appointments with you on their schedule. This is particularly helpful when using an autoresponder, as you can say something like, "Thanks for subscribing to my website. If you ever need one on one help or have questions about my product, please go here to schedule an appointment." It helps you look busy and professional.

2. A blog — If you're a writer, having a blog helps keep your prospects informed about your business, your products and your life. It helps you establish that human connection. Blogs can also be about something other than your business. These blogs might discuss a recent birdwatching trip you went on or your last mountain biking adventure. Believe it or not, blogs about your interests will attract followers and if worked right can generate leads using autoresponders.

3. A Daily Method of Operation — In my last book, I shared what I use as a DMO (see below). This helps with consistency, tracking the people I am meeting with and what their objections are. You can the downloadable one found on my website under Blog tab, or create your own.

White Wave Asea	WORK SCHEDULE					Week of May 5, 2014
TASK	Mon	Tue	Wed	Thur	Fri	Weekend
Business Tasks (filing, email, books)	9-10	9-10	9-10	9-10	9-10	
Phone Calls to Leads	10-10:30	10-10:30	10-10:30	10-10:30	10-10:30	
Who?						
Follow-Up Schedule (with whom, when?)						
Follow-Up Call Made (who)						
Contact existing partners/customers	10:30-11	10:30-11	10:30-11	10:30-11	10:30-11	
Who? How?						
Build New Leads	11:00-12	11:00-12	11:00-12	11:00-12	11:00-12	
What Was Done?						
Clubs	1 hour		1 hour		1 hour	
Which One						
Events	2 hours		2 hours		2 hours	
Which One						
Motivational Study		1 hour		1 hour		
What was done?						
Social Media	1 Hour	1 hour		1 hour		
Which Ones						
Charge Up/Vision Call	1 hour	1 hour	1 hour	1 hour	1 hour	
What I Learned/Anecdote						

4. A subscription to a service that helps you keep track of upcoming events in your area. This is super important, as it will help you find the sort of events you could go to and perhaps generate some friendships. I am talking something above and beyond Meetup®, though Meetup® can be very useful for this. I'm thinking something like a local newsletter or membership in the Chamber of Commerce. You never know when something will catch your eye and result in that DHE (dedicated, hardworking and experienced) network marketer.

5. A coach to help you with your weak points. Yes, this is a time for a shameless plug. I am available for one-one-one consulting. You can choose the program that suits you best on my website www.networkmarketingforintroverts.com under "Services." Once you've signed up, you will receive an invitation to make an appointment with me, worksheets and some of the material I've mentioned in this book.

If you feel okay as an introvert, but need to work on another issue, Google "coaches" and name your weak points. Then be willing to pay what is necessary to get past whatever it is. I promise you it will be worth it.

Manage your relationships

While network marketing means you never have to work alone, it is also important to remember that you get in life what you tolerate. Tolerate a pushy extrovert and you'll get pushed so much you eventually lose interest in a serious improvement to your nest egg. Tolerate inefficiency and things grow more inefficient. Tolerate people who make excuses and you get more excuses. Tolerate negativity and you get more negatives, and it just keeps compounding, day after day, year after year, until you have nothing but zeroes in your life. You wouldn't bank somewhere if their interest rate compounded in reverse, reducing your investment instead of growing it, would you? So let them go, those drains on your energy. Stop trying to change the downline who is no more than a glorified customer. Move on to the person who is serious about their future.

In the three short years I've been in the industry, I've learned that network marketing is truly a numbers game. It is essential that you keep building your list, employing every tool at your disposal, including those found in this book and those recommended by your company to the extent you can. Sometimes the people you're sure will be awesome in this business aren't, while the people you thought would stink at it blow your mind. If you can swing making at least 33% of your contacts come to fruition, you're on your way. If you don't, ask for help, ask for leads, ask for three-way calls, ask for encouragement, and don't be shy about asking for space to recharge your batteries (see previous chapter for some talking points when dealing with your extroverted team mates). If your team is in this for mutual benefit, every relationship in every direction should be a two-way street. Honor those relationships as you would a valued friendship. After all, even those members of your team who sometimes rub you the wrong way are contributing to your success.

Maintain your momentum

Make your work day count by staying in what psychologists call "the flow." Flow is when one pursues an activity for its own sake, not for the rewards it brings. In a "flow," one can work effortlessly for hours without distraction and remain persistent, even consistent, without worrying about outcome. It is a stone cold fact that if you only work your business sporadically, you may never build a successful business. Even if you can only work your business three hours a day, make those hours a regular habit. Don't let anything interrupt the pattern. The universe rewards steady, concentrated effort.

If you find yourself beginning to move out of your flow, redirect your activity to something meaningful. For a network marketer, especially an introvert, one must be vigilant against things that tell you they have meaning but don't, like organizing your pencils and pens by color. If it is meaningful, it will move you toward your goals, without being about the reward of achieving them. For example, consistently making calls and building your list is meaningful and keeps you in the flow. Doing the same with the idea that you'll make a sale every third call takes you out of the flow.

Remember my old boss at the burger joint? Peck knew he had to follow the model Orange Julius provided. He had been trained that so many burgers meant the life of his business. So ask yourself, "If I would get fired for not making five calls today, would I be willing to make them?" Weigh the benefits of staying focused against the instant gratification of your bad habits. Give yourself an "atta girl" (or "atta boy") and keep going no matter how far up the ranks you rise. Even at the top when it is possible to take a breather, don't rest too long or your engine will be cold and your momentum will be stopped.

As long as we're discussing consistent effort, let me make it clear that I do not mean boring effort. Switch things around, stretch your legs, do something you never tried before, all in the service of keeping momentum going. Getting bored can be just as much of a momentum killer as stopping all together.

The truth is, momentum can be destroyed by all kinds of things. Boredom, fear of success, jealousy, frustration, reaching a goal, even certain people can stop your business in its tracks. Make a commitment to stay in the flow so your momentum is continuous. If it means pulling away from people who are negative, unreliable or make excuses, do so.

You can succeed in this business if you do just one thing!

Good things happen to people who keep their promises, because their aura reflects self-confidence. However, that feeling starts with keeping the commitments you make to the one person you can't lie to: yourself!

Being a man or woman of your word will do more to draw people to you than anything else in this book. Start by recognizing this is going to take some time; you just have to commit to making sure it happens. That means planning well, using tools, building your list, working consistently and following through. While at times the task may seem daunting, one can turn that around by deciding here and now to drive yourself forward, regardless of how hard it may seem at times.

You may have heard of the Law of Attraction. This immutable law only works if accompanied by another law of the Universe: The Law of Perception. If you look at network marketing like an onerous, daunting and miserable job, that is what you will attract. If you look at network marketing like a sometimes challenging but ultimately rewarding path to financial freedom, that is what you'll get. In addition, if you perceive the promises you make to yourself as "optional," then your relationships with other people's promises will be optional and have disappointing results.

When you keep promises you feel good and that in turn generates a kind of self-confidence that cannot be shaken by disappointment and doubt. Soon that self-confidence helps others perceive you in a way that's destined to bring success to your efforts. Not every time, but most of the time. Soon the combination of your self-confidence and your commitment to your promises will start an unstoppable flood of new leads. People like to be on a winning team. Show them you can be a leader by modeling the behaviors it takes to be a success.

So promise yourself that you'll make those calls, write those emails, build those landing pages, acquaint yourself with technology, build your list, partner up and follow up.

The promises you keep to yourself will be reflected in the fulfillment of promises you make to others. Be brave, be stalwart, be committed to your network marketing success. After all, this is your business, your responsibility, to make of it what you want it to be. So ask yourself: what do I want my business to be and what am I willing to do to get it there? When you've determined what that is, set a course to make it so. Keep the promises you've made and the sky's only the beginning.

A Manifesto for Introverts
By Susan Cain

1. There's a word for 'people who are in their heads too much': thinkers.
2. Solitude is a catalyst for innovation.
3. The next generation of quiet kids can and must be raised to know their own strengths.
4. Sometimes it helps to be a pretend extrovert. There will always be time to be quiet later.
5. But in the long run, staying true to your temperament is key to finding work you love and work that matters.
6. One genuine new relationship is worth a fistful of business cards.
7. It's OK to cross the street to avoid making small talk.
8. 'Quiet leadership' is not an oxymoron.
9. Love is essential; gregariousness is optional.
10. 'In a gentle way, you can shake the world.' - Mahatma Gandhi"

Bibliography. Great Reads to Help You in the Process

Titles that are starred are essential if you're looking to succeed. *

Adler, Jordan	*Beach Money*
Anastasi, Mark	*The Laptop Millionaire**
Ancowitz, Nancy	*Self-promotion for Introverts*
Arbinger Institute	*The Anatomy of Peace**
Bateman, Kody	*MLM Blueprint; Your Subconscious Journey to Network Marketing Success**
Blanchard, Ken	*Lead with Luv (with Colleen Barrett)*
Bristol, Claude	*TNT: The Power Within You*
Brown, Brene	*The Gifts of Imperfection**
Bucholtz, Ester	*The Call of Solitude*
Cain, Susan	*Quiet: The Power of Introverts in a World That Can't Stop Talking**
Carnegie, Dale	*How to Win Friends and Influence People*
Covey, Stephen	*7 Habits of Highly Effective Network Marketing Professionals*
Covey, Stephen	*7 Habits of Highly Effective People*
Elsberg, Sandy	*Bread Winner, Bread Baker*
Fenton, Richard	*Go for No**
Hardy, Darren	*The Compound Effect**
Helgoe, Laurie	*Introvert Power: Why Your Inner Life is Your Hidden Strength**
Hensley, Dennis	*The Power of Positive Productivity*
Hill, Napoleon	*Think and Grow Rich*
Hood, Jenifer Kay	*Network Marketing for Introverts**
Kiyosaki, Robert	*The Cash Flow Quadrant*
Lupkin, Jim	*Network Marketing for Facebook®**
Lynch, Margaret	*Tapping Into Wealth**

Maltz, Maxwell	*Psycho-cybernetics**
Maltz, Maxwell	*Zero Resistance Selling*
Maxwell, John C.	*Put Your Dream to the Test: 10 Questions to Help You See It & Seize It*
Olson, Jeff	*The Slight Edge*
Peters, Tom	*In Search of Excellence*
Pritchard, Paula	*Owning Yourself**
Rohn, Jim	*Building Your Business**
Rohn, Jim	*The Five Major Pieces to the Life Puzzle*
Rohn, Jim	*12 Pillars (with Chris Widener)*
Sandberg, Sheryl	*Lean In*
Sirolli, Ernesto	*Ripples from the Zambezi*
Shapiro, Steve	*Listening for Success**
Solis, Brian	*Engage: The Complete Guide for Brands and Businesses to Build, Cultivate and Measure Success in the New Web*
Tracy, Brian	*The Miracle of Self-Discipline: The No Excuses Way of Getting Things Done**
Tracy, Brian	*Change Your Mind, Change Your Life**
Ury, William	*Getting to Yes**
Worre, Eric	*Go Pro: 7 Steps to Becoming a Network Marketing Professional**
Zach, Devora	*Networking for People Who Hate Networking**
Ziglar, Zig	*See You At the Top!*

Glossary

While by no means complete, this Glossary should help you quickly understand words that may be unfamiliar to you.

AUTORESPONDER — A service that allows visitors to your website or landing page automatically receive a response when they contact you looking for something. If they subscribe, it thanks them for their subscription. If they order a free digitized gift, it sends it to them. In the process the autoresponder captures the names and contact information you require and keeps a record of everyone who visited your site. Common autoresponder services are: Aweber, Constant Contact, Mail Chimp and Infusionsoft.

BOOKMARKLET — An app that allows you to "book mark" a website or blog post to be used later for future content on your Pinterest®, Tumblr® or other social media page.

DOWNLINE — The person below you on the compensation tree.

EMOTICONS — Emoticons are little symbol and letter combinations that "spell" something emotional. This ;=) spells "wink, happy" and receives a 52% higher interaction rate than spelling out the emotion. Some emoticons get a greater response than others. For example, :D (big smile) and :P (tongue hanging out) get 2.4 X and 2 X higher response rates respectively than a simple smiley.

KEYWORD — Back in the day, keywords were all the rage. Today, neither Google or Bing use keywords to determine a site's ranking in search results. However, some smaller search engines use them in their algorithm, so it might be worth it to add them just in case. Keywords are the words most commonly used when searching for information about something. For example, let's say you were looking up "network marketing for introverts" on Google. The keywords there are network marketing and introverts. In addition to my book (I hope!), you will find anything about introverts and network marketing. Some of it will be relevant to introverts, some won't be. Like a website that says, "introverts can't be network marketers." Keywords should be listed in a conversational style, just the way you'd say it if you were speaking with someone in a hurry, like screaming, "lettuce" at your husband as he pulls out of the driveway on his way to the grocery store. Don't just jam a bunch of words in there for the sake of listing them (lettuce, romaine, butter, iceberg, red leaf, kale). It won't help anyone find you any faster. Incidentally, you'll have to understand basic HTML to put keywords into your post. Ironically, you can find out how to do that using Google or Bing. By the way, keywords are invisible to people visiting your site and should be the same as the tags you're using in an article or blog post.

META DESCRIPTION — You know those little short descriptions you find when you Google something, the ones with the words in your search in bold? That's a meta description. A meta description should be between 100 and 150 characters, offer a valuable, compelling reason why someone should visit the page (something like "Consumer Reports best buy soap"), and use both the primary and secondary keyword you're aiming for in the blog post. You'll need to know HTML or have an app supplied by your blog provider that allows you to simply insert a description for improving your search engine ranking.

TAGS — WordPress calls these "categories" (as do some other blog sites). Tags summarize the topic of the blog post, like a tab in a filing system. For example, your blog post might be, "My trip to St. Thomas." The tags might be "travel" and "Caribbean." The keywords might be "tropical" and "Virgin Islands." Use tags to make it simple for your followers to find a topic they're interested in. Put no more than three tags per blog post.

SEO — Search Engine Optimization. The process by which one positions their blog or website through tags, keywords and meta descriptions to bring it to the top of search engines like Google or Bing.

UPLINE — The person who sponsored you and anyone above them in the organizational tree.

Url — Stands for Uniform Resource Locator. A website address, such as **www.networkmarketingforintroverts.com**, is a url. Sometimes written in all caps, like URL.

www.ingramcontent.com/pod-product-compliance
Lightning Source LLC
Chambersburg PA
CBHW070239190526

45169CB00001B/235